WHAT LOVE COMES TO

BOOKS BY RUTH STONE

RUTH STONE

What Love Comes To

New & Selected Poems

Foreword by Sharon Olds

 Copper Canyon Press
Port Townsend, Washington

Cover art: Susan Bennerstrom, *Twisp*, 2005. Oil pastel on panel, 40" × 48".

Copper Canyon Press gratefully acknowledges Southern Illinois University Press for the reproduction of Sharon Olds's essay from *The House Is Made of Poetry: The Art of Ruth Stone.*

Copper Canyon Press is in residence at Fort Worden State Park in Port Townsend, Washington, under the auspices of Centrum. Centrum is a gathering place for artists and creative thinkers from around the world, students of all ages and backgrounds, and audiences seeking extraordinary cultural enrichment.

LIBRARY OF CONGRESS CATALOGING-IN-PUBLICATION DATA

Stone, Ruth.
What love comes to: new and selected poems / Ruth Stone.
   p. cm.
ISBN 978-1-55659-271-3 (cloth: alk. paper)
I. Title.
PS3537.T6817W47 2008
811'.54—dc22

                                           2007045832

9 8 7 6 5 4 3 2 FIRST PRINTING

COPPER CANYON PRESS
Post Office Box 271
Port Townsend, Washington 98368
www.coppercanyonpress.org

Dedicated to Don Croll

August 19, 1939–January 11, 2008

Beloved father of my grandchildren Nora Swan, Jesse Ehsan,
and Sahara Najat; world traveler, lover of the Persian language,
and my dear friend for over fifty years.

⌐

For some we loved, the loveliest and the best
That from his Vintage rolling Time hath prest,
    Have drunk their Cup a Round or two before,
And one by one crept silently to rest.

The Rubáiyát of Omar Khayyám

CONTENTS

NEW POEMS

What Love Comes To   (2008)

FROM

Cheap: New Poems and Ballads   (1975)

FROM

Second-Hand Coat: Poems New and Selected   (1987)

FROM

Who Is the Widow's Muse?   (1991)

FROM

Simplicity (1995)

FROM

Ordinary Words (1999)

FROM

In the Next Galaxy (2002)

FROM

In the Dark   (2004)

Ruth Stone and Her Poems

A Ruth Stone poem feels alive in the hands — ardent, independent, restless. A Stone poem propels forward like a gifted wide receiver — it has "broken field" (the ability to change course, instantly, at speed, left or right, with great precision); it swivels its hips and *moves*.

Ruth Stone's poems are mysterious, hilarious, powerful. They are understandable, often with a very clear surface, but not simple — their intelligence is crackling and complex. Her poems are musical, and their music is unforced, unlabored-over, fresh.

In my midteens I had the joy of meeting Ruth Stone, and in my late teens and early twenties I had the blessing of visiting Ruth and her daughters in Vermont. She gave me a vision of a genius at work. She herself seemed to be the location of a *daimon;* she was a place where life turned into art. She was a woman who chopped wood for hearth fires and hauled water, in winter, from the river — first hacking a hole in the ice with an ax. She was a great beauty (with a great West Virginia melodious mountain cackle) who wore old softened blue jeans and men's (one beloved man's) Oxford shirts. The beam of her attention was extremely bright, warm, and encouraging, and she was *in love with* poetry.

I saw her living a life of poetry that was communal — not that she sought readers out in the greater world; she did not seem to send poems to magazines, or books to publishers — but readers were there, in the living room, in Brandon, Vermont. When you were there you felt yourself to be in the heart of the poetry family.

The great sweeping beams of her eyes, the great sweeping beams of her heart, softly raked the earth, the house. Her senses seemed acute as an owl's. In one way she seemed the persona of a shapely warm-blooded small mammal, a snowy marten, perhaps,

or a snowshoe hare — not a predator but one of the predated up-
on — but as a poet she was a great hunter, noiseless, keen, joyful,
beautiful, rakish and eerie by moonlight, and her poems were alive,
vivid: *they* were the owls. (Now I remember that there was an owl
in that house — a stuffed owl, in the study of her late husband,
the poet Walter Stone. When I saw it I thought of a revenant, and
of Minerva, goddess of knowledge sought and unsought.)

One blizzardy Christmas I spent in Vermont with Ruth and
her family. What larks! I love the pair of pink waffled cotton
bloomers that were one of the treats in my stocking (which had
a felt hearth, and felt fire, and felt candelabra on it). Every day
for hours we'd play the Poetry Game — everyone would think up
one word, then we'd pool them, then we'd write poems each of
which contained all the pooled words. The food and the dishes
would run out at about the same time, and we'd keep going on
tea and imagery.

Ruth, a great, generous appreciator, could see the spark of life
in each poem. I remember her ferocious doting *attention* when
one read, her childlike pleasure and focus, her joy in poetry, her
need of it, and the beauty of her body, girlish and voluptuous, as
she sat and listened — and her catty humor, and her wonder.

She is a poet of tragedy, and she is a jaunty poet, not proper,
her work without middle-class prudishness. She is a poet of great
humor — mockery even — and a bold eye, not obedient. There is
a disrespect in her poems, a taken freedom, that feels to me like
a strength of the disenfranchised.

Ruth's poems are direct and lissome, her plainness is elegant
and shapely, her music is basic, classical; it feels as real as the
movement of matter. When we hear a Stone first line, it is as if
we have been hearing this voice in our head all day, and just now
the words become audible. She is a seer, easily speaking clear
truths somehow unmentioned until now. And one has the sense
of enough air in her poems — they lift up.

I love Ruth Stone's irony, and the melody of her irony. In many of her poems we hear the music of the quiet, deep unhopefulness of the poor, the unfooled.

The things in Stone's poems are often ordinary and transcendent at the same time. Ruth has a kind of bald religious sense that is also political. She has sometimes the sound of a prophet. She gives us visions of the uses of power. She looks at the police, and the academics; she looks at gender and race and class, and she judges. They are the judgments of one who had had higher hopes for the human.

Ruth Stone also "dance[s] the diddy on a wrinkled knee" (*In an Iridescent Time*) — she has a lovely quality that approaches the silly, the "dirty." She has, sometimes, something of a snicker, a mocking note about sex. Her sharp focus is not blurred by ladylikeness. She has a canny lack of respect; she makes fun of what is pompous. Sometimes her making fun is slightly merciless, or bitter — a tit-for-tat sharpness toward a male academic, or a male surgeon. She has a savage cosmic vision. Her savagery is often feminist savagery — she is always for the earth, for the harmed mother.

Stone is bold and rich in describing the plants and things of the earth, and she does not overdescribe them so that they become literary artifacts rather than natural things. When she transplants them to the page, they keep their size and shape, and their roots don't die — she recognizes their principle of integrity, so their livingness survives over.

Stone has the image imagination. She seems to think in images, to easily visualize the invisible. She has a tragic deadpan humor: love and destruction are right next to each other.

Ruth Stone's voice is unsentimental. She has tremendous accuracy, tremendous pleasure in the thing-as-it-is, even when it is unpleasant, ridiculous, pathetic. And the *things* that dance in her books! The filing cases of wizened eggs! The furnaces!

In Ruth Stone's work there is wisdom, and there is reckless ballading. There is a lack of fear of the grotesque — mortality makes for the grotesque.

The premises of many of the poems are unusual. Often, their domestic location is fresh. And she has a vision of the bazook — she gives us the grim humor of ordinary awful misery. Ruth Stone strikes me as hilariously and seriously anti–middle class, seeing through class pretensions and refusals. Sometimes her poems go into a daring realm almost of nonsense talk — sometimes she Does Nonsense. It embodies the foolishness of hope, the stupidity of vanity and orderliness. One approaches, in it, the outskirts of a huge bitterness, which sings.

From the earliest poems, we see her effortless gift for musical language. Over time, the music has become more and more complex, as if she dances with her brain as much as with her feet. So much necessity came along, in her imagination and her subjects, and her art was so equal to it, that the poems were compressed into a severe tragic-comic genius; they often remind me of matter transformed by forces in the natural world. Stone seems to have a deeply grounded sense of space and time. She gives enough time to the colloquial sentence; she lets it stretch out and have its natural time along the lines. She has a fine sense of how long things take, of duration — how time feels, passing.

Ruth Stone's poems, in their originality and radiance, their intelligence and music and intense personal politics, shine in their place within her generation, among the pioneering women (Bishop, Brooks, Rukeyser). Her unusual lack of self-promotion has resulted in her work being slow to find its readers. But her readers are passionate in their respect and love and amazement over her poems — the poems' energy, freshness, and spunk, their speaking to our lives. This volume should help more of us find her; we are hungry for her. Ruth Stone's poems are the food the spirit craves, the lasting nourishment Louise Bogan referred to when she said, "Here's a crumb of hereafter." Stone gives us loaves and loaves of hereafter, of Adamant here and now.

Sharon Olds

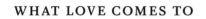

WHAT LOVE COMES TO

NEW POEMS

What Love Comes To

2008

Tendrils

While leaves are popping bullets of air,
they are saying something—
a flux of otherness,
a pulse of organic sex.
But the wind sucks up
the slightest moth
or spider that leaps
throwing its web in the shadows—
a continuous tongue of foreign talk.
It is a matriarchy,
perhaps a grandmother,
vast and all knowing, this caster
of violent,
untranslatable language.

The Alien

Like myself, the body gets in bed.
Unlike myself, it reads blank words, blank books.
I know I'm not,
but I suspect I'm dead.

Some message on a wall erased by rain.
Some house, some street, some other place;
behind me salt dissolving salt;
and where I step I cannot step again.

Now the body rises to be fed.
It knows its own.
It does not need my codes or maps.
It does not care what's hanging in my head.

The Old Story

Although he didn't
love me, I loved him.
Most wives know this
story; the patience
of midnight.
It was the same with
my mother and father.
My father, yes, he
gambled, he gave
jewelry to other women.
After he died, my mother
bought a wristwatch
for herself and a small
diamond engagement ring—
which she wore to church
or when she shopped
for groceries;
for those were her outings.
Perhaps she took them off
when she worked in the garden.
Her hands were slender,
she wore gloves when
she dressed up.
After my father died she bought
a mohair couch and an
Oriental rug for the living room.
And even then
she wept for him.

Imprint of the Stereoscopic Cards

If you make a connection between this table and that table,
then you will remember your grandmother's loaves of bread
and from there you arrive outside the gates of Jerusalem.
Your jealous and unkind aunt Virginia, who is six years older
than you, has made it a rule that you must look at each card,
even that one of the lepers. Your grandmother knows nothing
        of this.
Rotting in rags, their voices crying, "Unclean, unclean."
The lepers' lips are eaten away. They hold out their stumps.
Bones come through their soiled wrappings.
And yet they are odorless on the stereoscopic cards.

Bread is made twice a week on the scrubbed kitchen table.
You are seven, waiting for the boxed tour of Jerusalem.
The trick of two eyes and two photographs.
Then your whole body enters into that place.
You take in your mouth the warm buttered bread
from your grandmother's white flowered hands.
You sit with the viewer; waiting to slide into focus
the lettered and numbered cards and to hold
for the rest of your life these cast-out bodies of lepers.

Setting Type

From a long way, the semicolon begins to wave.
"Hello!"
He's on the telephone.
"We were just passing en route, the period and I."
They are so cute.
"There's a half gallon of hearty burgundy," I say.
Are they having an affair?
"Well, the period's rather tired."
I forget how shy they are.
We're so glad to see one another
that we skip the long paragraphs between,
the deep pages of doubt,
but after a review, the material grows thin.
"I'm in another book now," I say.
We ink each other thoughtfully.
"You sure you'll be comfortable in these old journals?"
"Yes, yes. The fried vocabulary was good."
The next day they are off.
"Good punctuation," I say. "A nice pair.
I think they ought to get edited and settle down."

The Real Travelers

It was supposed to snow, but it rained
the last two weeks in March;
or is it a week and three days?
Whatever. No matter what groceries
you lay in, you are not hungry.
But you feel the rush of the body
through the thickening air—

although the folks next door
park their cars and turn on their TV,
and mysterious as mice,
something occurs between them.
And although they are short and dense
and curiously look like aliens;
they are professional cleaners
in other people's houses
and their tiny dog is not allowed
to bark at the window.
I ask, where are those birds?
On the other side of town,
my left brain answers.
I am so blind I can no longer see
the lines in my hands.
Now who will interpret me?
But it does not matter.

We lope along the galaxy,
along one thickening arm,
winking at Eta Carinae.

Blast away sister, we sigh,
as something ignites her furious hair.
Her bodies trembling like
bloated bellies of man-of-war jellyfish,
trailing their stinging colonies—
or the bursting bellies of spider's eggs,
ready to loft the baby spiders into orbit—
the real travelers starting out for Mars.

Work

The voice of the laundry says, hang me;
hang me, or I will mold.
The voice of the clothesline says,
tighter or I will sag.
The voice of the front porch says, sit here.
Tell me, what is the meaning of this?
While the subliminal shrews are ferociously
eating, always eating, in order to waste away.

From Where We Are

Embedded in the navel
of the belly of our goddess,
we are deeper in
and closer to her viscera.
That is why,
in the gurgles of her vast digestion,
we are shaken with thought waves
in her fiery pores, in the gluons
that flicker
in her infinite intestines,
pouring out of her
the eternal roar.
Our galaxies blink in the
skin of her navel
as we perceive her ecstatic curvature.

What It Comes To

Sometimes I cry for that young man
I loved fifty years ago. My, my, he has been
dead for almost half a century.
His voice trembled when he spoke to me.
What did I know of men and their cupidity?
And do I cry for myself,
that lonely, ignorant woman?
Not half, I think.
Even in my sleep I laugh,
a common sentiment.
The average cheap romance;
the family's dull drama.
But you—bone and skin that you are—
you didn't even want
to come to the desert without shoes.
Scorpions, snakes, thorns.
But there were the stars
and the breath of something, stamens,
the centers of the thinnest tissues;
the momentary
and almost tangible universe.

Memory

Can it be that
memory is useless,
like a torn web
hanging in the wind?

Sometimes it billows
out, a full high gauze—
like a canopy.

But the air passes
through the rents
and it falls again and flaps
shapeless
like the ghost rag that it is—

hanging at the window
of an empty room.

All in Time

I

With something to do,
no wonder I sit at the typewriter.
Behind me, the clock has the
monotonous voice of a parent.
Always it is something else I prefer.
The dictionary is a moving finger,
the compressed words of my life.
It's ridiculous, asparagus, asphodel,
accoutrements,
spine in alphabetical order.
More Pope than Pope,
also born hunchback
with a niggling spirit
it sends me a telegram saying,
"If you're close in Melrose, look me up.
You can find me under lexicon."

II

In the West End we could take a cab,
a cob, a Cadillac.
I run into town to send a hot wire
back up the mountain.
No category here by that name.
Suggest you try some party in Cincinnati,
Cryptos, Crimea.

III

Do you take my place
electron microscope?
Strip of film, blast off,
jet-lagged, space probed,
plastic velvet-lined motor,
sensor cube, in webby
hemispheres;
left right crossing the electric orb,
the bridge of sighs
from my winter to yours;
whispering, shrinking,
blank phonemes fading,
falling.

IV

The cement driller bends down
into the cavity of the street.
Gray gum of the sidewalk sprays from his drill.
Bombarded every day by neutrinos,
I walk down Longest Avenue holding my umbrella.
Information, merely information;
everywhere bone sparkle,
radials sifting deeper into ooze.
How I am coming apart.
How I scatter.
The air sparkles with my dust.

V

Little potato, dried Russian apple,
sweet-cheeked mama
with the singing broom,
I am not even good wine.
You've wasted your vats on me.
Flying snow queen in your wicker carriage
riding over the moon
and farther in those fairy tales,
when the clear morning star sailed in my bedroom window.
We were all barking
and the yellow jackets stung our bare feet
in the deep clover.
Lamps, like those lamps in the evening parlor,
come and go in secondhand shops.
Even the panorama photographs of
between the wars,
and no one laughs that way anymore.

VI

My unknown, my own skeleton,
you will take me where the cartilage loosens
and the blood dries
and I will let go
my burning suns.
I am not Helen,
I die with Carthage.
I see carnage in man.
I dissolve in your old useless salts.
Love and fear attracted my double helix,
broke bonds with me.
Neither man nor woman,

but I remain until then
your singular subject.

VII

Violent creatures of your island continent,
scattered, expelled by the giant
hunting you down,
we ride with our leaping kangaroo.

We are your embryos in the pouch of fire.
We hang out the windows of your brothy sack,
riding with you in the bushfire
under your ribs,
as we swing along the track of naked bullets.

VIII

The rattan lampshade sags
above the incense burner;
the cheap Victorian clock unwinds
like forgotten guilt;
ivy climbs the windows.
Here the embarrassing body,
wrapped in acrylic,
coaxes its thickened veins
and blood gathers in its bulging heart.

IX

I sort my reflections by their titillations,
a little pain, a little physical duress,
a teasing corner of oblivion.

My body, in the multiple stress of the moment,
ages and cracks.
The centipedes confess to finally forgetting which end was first.
The primal fire expands into the inner bubble
of the universe.

Sir William Hershel saw pinpoints
of another kind of space
from which the milk of galaxies was poured,
as from a pitcher.
What is this universe that occupies my face?
I travel in an orderly erratic place.
I am a particle,
I am going toward something. I am complicated,
and yet, how simple is my verse.

     X

The top of the poplar is shaking out money,
but it will not fall.
As I am my own sister, it will fall;
as the sun has its humors, it will fall.
But now it tickles itself crying "poor, poor."
Light, controlling birds, dancing midges of light—
history never relents
spending and being spent.
Make heads and tails of this—
poets never make money.

XI

This language, given me from birth,
was not my language.
But in you, I knew a generous woman's voice.
You were puzzled, as I,
at the choices of death,
that we die at birth,
that we die as we are born,
denying ourselves and women.
Even you,
though you secretly gave me one eye which saw,
and one ear which heard.

XII

My father, as you had a shot at her,
you had a shot at me.
My father, as I am your child,
I am the diseased prostitute.
The vessel apart from you;
the container.
As the choir of undescended boys sings of God, the father,
so I sing of my mother—
as the apostles, as the defiled.
Out of this, we come in the endless sadness of children.

But You're Only Sleeping on the Bus

One morning you wake up in a trailer
on the Moline River.
Never mind how you got here.
You crack open a wine cooler,
slop around in your pink scuffs.
Fishing pole and semiautomatic
beside the door. You look down.
Your housecoat is smeared with it.
You feel your nose. It is swollen.
You pick at the dried blood.
The indoor-outdoor carpet
stinks of his piss, unmistakable.
Razor strop on the bathroom wall,
unsheathed razor in there; switchblade.
KKK cuff links scattered alongside
his La-Z-Boy. You know by osmosis
the shape of the dark ten-by-ten
with king-size bed back there
off the plywood wall. This is not
virtual reality. You listen for his snore.
Nothing but silence. He sprawls,
Levi's half off, belt on the floor, where
he went down in his vomit
across the chenille spread.
At the teasing edge you begin to remember
something; another place.
Your chest is knocking like a trapped ferret.
Now you remember. He's dead.

For the Dead

At night you look at me
from your ivory sockets,
as if this mistake had
never been made;
as if the feral blood
still served.
A body laid out
on a rusty scuttle,
in a brittle cage,
you probe like a white rat
looking for openings;
the buzzer,
your dismembered ecstasy.

Eta Carinae

The snow coming straight down
like heavy rain,
the crows protesting—
what do they know?
So the weather patterns change.
The crows, blue jays,
the soggy robins, the goldfinches—
dupes of the weather,
all deceived by the light.
The sun, wobbling and coughing
along the dust belt;
the entire galaxy
shuddering with Eta Carinae
swollen to term.
The supernovae, like Christ,
come to illuminate the ignorant,
who can only swallow one another.

Strings

We pop into life the way
particles pop in and out
of the continuum.
We are a seething mass
of probability.
And probably I love you.
The evil of larvae
and the evil of stars
are a formula for the future.
Some bodies can
thrust their arms into
a flame and be instantly
cured of this world,
while others sicken.
Why think, little brother
like the moon, spit out like
a broken tooth.
"Oh," groans the world.
The outer planets,
the fizzing sun, here we come
with our luggage.
Look at the clever things
we have made out of
a few building blocks—
O fabulous continuum.

Immolation

Now the widow is mad.
If she smoked cigarettes,
she'd stub one out on her arm.
But she doesn't smoke.
"This is pure shit," she says.
And she thinks she'll get a tattoo.
One blue and one bright green breast.
And maybe on one buttock
a glass slipper.
The muse is having a joint.
The muse is depressed.

Speaking to My Dead Mother

At two A.M. in Binghamton, it's quiet.
I did not comfort you with one last kiss.
Your death was my death. Instinct ran riot.
I ran. Didn't hold your hand at the abyss.
My life had gone like grass fire; like the trees
in drought, caught in the burning wind. And June
returns, another cycled year. Sweet-peas,
dahlias, phlox; the orchard I can't prune;
your small garden gloves, remnants of crystal
stemware. It wears away. I cannot bar
the passage. Jewelweed shoots its pistol
pouch of seeds and the storm, like a guitar,
thrums over the mountain. All that brooded,
ignorant in your safe arms, concluded.

The Basic Question

Are you then she,
the mother of my mother's
mother's mother,
nameless to me?
Are these hands like yours,
or these feet?
Anonymous, a mother
among the long braid
of mothers; among
the separate segments;
are you she?

Gone

Now fragmented as any bomb,
I make no lasting pattern;
and my ear, not cut off
in the logic of a van Gogh,
an offering of angry love,
is merely blown to bits
in a passing wave of violence.
Therefore I hear such fragments
as make no meaning.
A theater of the ridiculous,
beyond the absurd
and beyond that, scattered—
not like stars, but like the coalescing
weight of gravity; thin and meaningless,
until, tenuous, like the finest web
stretched out, it collapses and carries all
into a single disappearing zero.

Monetary Problems

The widow goes to the bank.
She needs a new roof,
or a new house; whichever.
Janet, the young woman in loans,
gives her the forms to fill out.
The print is small.
The spaces are small.
The widow tries to feel confident.
Social Security isn't much
but it's certainly something, she says.
Janet is busy, busy,
but she takes the ninety-seven
for the appraisal.
After a month the bank inspects the place.
Substandard, the bank says,
keeping the ninety-seven.
No fixed income.
Too much of a risk.
Perhaps if the widow had a brother
or a son-in-law to cosign.
That was just a gender suggestion,
of course, the muse says.

The Follies of My Youth

It's taken me eighty-five years
to become mediocre.
How brilliant I was;
how I threw it away like used Kleenex.
I never walked the side streets of New York,
I never played tennis,
I never swam in the Olympic pool—
I know my boundaries.

My neighbor's daughter
married into the Hogg Drugstore
and died of uterine cancer at thirty.
What was all that for?
At a party given by this new rich family
I ignored my partner, the short brother.
The short brother and the tall brother
were twins. I wanted to dance with the tall one.
The short one went inside and cried.
His mother made cruel remarks about me.

Could I have done the same as the neighbor's daughter,
married the short Hogg brother, and died young, too?
Here I am, old and poor.
Where is that short twin now?
Where is his loyal mother?
But I didn't think of bettering myself;
there were too many books in the world.
There was so much I wanted to read.

The Dorm

I know the violence of hormones—adrenaline.
Along these halls at night,
doors explode with the hoarse screams
of young men;
their cartilage bursting at seams;
manic, they run barefoot,
throwing banana skins,
pounding on walls,
laughing hysterically—
and the screams of young women
pitched like sirens,
racing to blood,
to disaster,
slamming doors;
the fierce hoots of their stereos
flooding the savage arteries
with a thumping manual of themselves.
Their eyes, when I pass them by day,
bitter as warriors
after a week of poison and flagellation.
In the morning, as after some public funeral,
or shocking event,
corridors strewn with torn paper
like skin;
flesh-colored crusts of pizza,
smashed records,
beer bottles slammed into powdered glass,
but empty and dim

with a hospital silence—
an odor like ether or alcohol,
as in the healing nature of a strictured wound.

Sin

I remember a Harvard student,
who couldn't admit to himself
that he was gay,
suddenly one day
telling everyone
he was a lampshade.
He was so convinced
he tried to stick his fingers
into wall sockets.
The ambulance squad
wrapped him in a straitjacket
and drove him away.

Somewhere he may be lighting
someone's darkness—
whatever—
More likely,
he is still a lampshade,
a lampshade pressed tight
upon a hot bulb,
a lampshade—perhaps accordion pleated—
as they used to be—
in the opulent fifties
after the Second World War,
when factories turned
back to confetti
and women took off
their overalls.

Poor boy,
he only wanted
to love some man—
who knows who?
And speaking of real sin,
we had just dropped
that bomb on Japan
and radiation
was two miles high—
just dust in the blue.

A Leap in Memory

My sister's blue iris grows
near the corner of the porch,
my mother's phlox nearby;
the lilacs from the Vassar campus
near the fallen barn.
Each spring,
with the squills and ancient
apple trees—
the air is a chorus of pollinators.
Frogs, the size of fingernails,
shrill from swamp to tree;
they cross the road
in vast, compulsive
migrations, bulging eyes
and throbbing throats—
or by the thousands they die
under the wheels of cars.

The Dog

The dog is God.
It knows it is God.
It is God living with God.
Even in the rain,
the esters, the pheromones,
calligraphy of the sacred,
the great head points into the wind,
the blood thrashes in the thick veins.
The language of the feces, urine,
species, rut, offal, decay—
nothing is hidden from the dog,
who keeps its own counsel,
leading you by the leash.

Why I Left California

Mildred's mother gave me an umbrella for Christmas.
That was about all I got.
Of course, I wasn't one of the family,
and Mildred was paying the rent.
The rich find it hard to tolerate too much of that.
I couldn't find a job.
The umbrella was see-through plastic with green dots,
but in Sierra Beach it never seemed to rain.

Mildred's mother was about eighty
and she had a widow's hump,
a lump of fat between her shoulder blades.
Her dresses had to be altered
to fit this little fat on her back.
Mildred offered me her mother's retired clothes,
which were from the best California shops.
Shantung or raw silk,
always carefully pressed and just back from the cleaners.
They looked good on the hanger,
but my New England bones
couldn't accommodate that widow's hump.

Mildred asked me to come out and live with her
because she wasn't well.
She kept getting tooth infections,
pneumonia and other things.
For years she had been a sophisticated,
adolescent, Shirley Temple–type beauty,
a young Madame Alexander real living doll.

She was a working writer,
she reported for big-time New York magazines,
like *Esquire.*
She was pumped full of brains and estrogen.
She never grew any older physically.
She was Peter Pan in drag.
But then, her teeth began to give her trouble,
and she got involved with a big-time dentist.
Whatever she did,
Mildred always got involved with the head honcho.
On the set of a movie she was covering,
she would get involved with the director.
Her flirtation with the dentist had ended
and he gave her a nagging bill.
Her love affair, in the dentist chair,
developed a dry socket.
It was getting toward winter,
her jobs had slacked off,
and she suddenly wanted to go back to her origins.
San Loze, California, a zippy small town of grand houses
and swimming pools, the country clubs and lawyers,
who were friends of the family
and vice presidents with stocks in old organizations,
like canned milk.
Not movies, but real society and the Yacht Club.
But then she ended up in Sierra Beach
because her sister lived on an island nearby,
and she basically hated her sister,
which made her sister a substitute
for the aching tooth.
Mildred always needed something to harangue about.

The night the earthquake knocked my bed around the room,
there was an eclipse.
I stayed up to watch Earth's shadow.
A blot of black spilling slowly across the moon.
I lay on a lounge out on the patio
and looked at the dark shadow of Earth crossing the sky
like a prehistoric bird swallowing the full disk.
The air was heavy with jasmine and roses
and I knew those bird-of-paradise flowers were out there
with their scarlet beak blossoms.
All that afternoon I had lain back watching the passing
        monarch butterflies,
in flocks quite big and migrating.
In the anticlimax following the eclipse,
I could finally see again
the silver of the moon on the water,
flickering far down the hill,
the water of the Pacific
in the clasped arms of the lagoon,
the semicircle of sand and gardens that were slowly being
        eaten away
by the surf and tides.
The house Mildred was renting was at the top of the hill,
overlooking the town of Sierra Beach.
Sometimes the yellow pollution thickened the air
and lay out on the Pacific like rolled-up batting,
ready to come in with the tide
and spread its acid throat-burning smog.
Then Mildred and I would close the doors and windows
and turn on the fans.
But the night of the eclipse was clear.

One of my jobs was to keep the fire going.
Mildred thought that the small iron stove leaked gas,
but here it was necessary on chilly damp days.
The wood was sort of brush,
stacked in the narrow slit between our fence and the house.
I squeezed into this lichen-slick niche and gathered the wood.
There was a continuous dialogue
between Mildred and the owner of the house
about whether the long metal pipe
that rose to the high ceiling
and then fit into a ceramic chimney on the roof
leaked gas.
I was used to wood-burning stoves.
I had one back in Vermont.
I felt Mildred's fears were ridiculous.
But she had an almost masculine side to her.
It would emerge in the voice of authority
and sometimes several tones deeper than her Shirley Temple voice.
Anyway, no smoke leaked out,
but Mildred was prone to engaging in vendettas.

The earthquake merged like cinema into the eclipse.
It was all part of the celluloid dream,
the early morning; still asleep,
I heard the rocks grind under the house.
My bed danced around the room.
It was my first earthquake
but I recognized it instantly.
There were equally strong aftershocks all day long.
The quake seemed like a novelty at first,
but that was my shock.
As the day wore on,
fear and reality became one.

I felt terror.
Buildings had collapsed on top of people.
Overpasses came down on cars.
People who live in California are used to this.
They clean it up and get on.
But after a few days,
I thought I would go back home.
The smog was dark. I was still nervous.
The place felt like an eggshell.
The foundations of the house had shaken apart.
The big rocks were all askew.
I got my bus ticket and packed my few things.
Mildred had instantly invited Woo to come and stay with her.
Woo drove me to the bus station.
The Santa Ana was blowing.

In the mountains, we ran into a snowstorm
that the bus driver couldn't handle,
but I felt right at home.
Although we had to stop over for one night
in a dreary roadside bus station,
I amused myself listening
to the passengers' sad stories.
Greyhound brings out the worst in everyone.
Nevertheless, I remained basically euphoric.
There were no snowplows,
but the snow melted and we went on through Arizona.
On and on, turning north toward New England,
I was happily pointed toward Eastern winter
and the simple hazards of icy roads and frostbite.
I was going home to the creosote and leaking gas
in my own stovepipes and my own woodpile.
Carefully taking with me my plastic umbrella.

The Porch

Whatsoever comes to the screen,
firefly or moth,
I lean back in the wicker chair,
the porch my fragile skin
between me
and the gorgeous open maw,
the sucking swallowing world.

Tsunami

At the solstice the Pacific Ocean sloshed
over the islands. Westward the terrified monkeys,
the red-faced ones, felt the earth tilt.
The ocean spilled like breast milk
into the submerged volcanoes.
As yet, the uncut forests in the highest
peaks are still inhabited by the tiniest spiders.
Their webs, flung and fastened
like elegant tailored buttonholes.
But all those on wings who came to drink,
with nothing under them, could only
capture moisture from the darkening air.

Fragrance

Edna St. Vincent Millay—
her friends called her Vincent—
lived for a time in New York,
in the Village.
E.E. Cummings lived there, too—
and even I was living then—
but in the Midwest,
in Indianapolis.

Then, my father,
sitting at his Linotype machine,
the hot lead slugs
clicking and falling,
would sometimes print
a poem of mine—
something he found
around the house.

Poems came to me
as if from far away.
I would feel them coming.
I would rush into the house,
looking for paper and pencil.
It had to be quick,
for they passed through me
and were gone forever.
What are children's poems?
Like the sudden breeze

that pulls the petals
from the honeysuckle.

Much later,
when I lived in the Village,
E.E. Cummings was a faint legend.
Poets come and go,
like squills that bloom
in the melting snow.

A Short History of My Brother

I ran ahead of them but my brother had run before me
and he hid behind the door so when I entered our house
in the dark, he jumped out and shouted boo. I fainted.
That was when they began to give me hot milk at bedtime
so I wouldn't shake. It was my little brother, my only brother,
Edgar A. Perkins. We called him Pete. A good kid.
He collected arrowheads. That night we had been to the Irving
      Theater.
Our mother had gone with us to see Rudolph Valentino
in *The Sheik.* I was madly in love with Valentino.
Even though he was dead. I've a talent for loving the dead.
It's easy to be faithful to the dead.
When you are caring for your only body,
bathing it, washing its hair, trimming its nails,
ignoring whatever is unpleasant and irreversible,
like a calendar hanging over the sink,
so that when you do the dishes, those appointments
and deadlines like the Serengeti lion on the flank of the wildebeest,
on the television, forever dying and yet never dead,
stare at you like the hidden half-suspected universe.
After the war my brother worked in the Composing Room,
like our father. He set headlines by hand for the daily *Star.*
He mourned the passing of the Linotype machine.
At home he sat on his patio working the daily crossword puzzle.
He went to church, gardened like our mother,
telling me he finally understood me
now that he was the father of two teenage girls.
His best suit had been stored in the closet
in a plastic bag in my mother's house, before he left for boot camp.

When he came home he discovered it had been riddled
by moths. Yes, my little brother, who twenty years ago
in the middle of a game of golf,
walked away from his friends and died alone in his car.
He lies in a mausoleum, the blue exhaust from traffic thickening
in a heavy layer as though an ancient ocean is slowly
filling the canyons of love in Indianapolis.

The Bungalow

To repeat this gossip—some neighbors made bathtub gin.
Mrs. Mix, our next-door neighbor, dyed her hair red;
had gentlemen friends during the week.
Our house was a bungalow. Between our house and theirs,
the sunlight scarcely warmed the slugs and snails,
the snails I found in the moss along the brick.
Mrs. Mix found Mr. Mix wedged between the bathtub and the wall.
Mr. Mix's funeral must have been held at the mortuary.
I don't remember it. Mrs. Mix grew cabbage roses.
She and my mother, when they met, were in the backyards
comparing their dahlia bulbs. We didn't have a car or a garage.
My father was not very tall. But he could run fast.
He often slept with the wrong women. In the evening we
would walk to the streetcar line. Sometimes our father would
come home. He was not very tall, but he was his mother's favorite.
He played the drums. When my father was sixteen he learned
to shoot craps on a riverboat. All the summers were long and hot.
Later we lived with him in a bungalow.
We lived with him and John Dillinger, Al Capone
and the Crash, in a bungalow. And without thinking, we children,
my brother and sister and I, had entered the history of the world.
After Hitler's army had goose-stepped over the desert,
after Normandy, after the war my father still sat at his Linotype
machine in the Composing Room of the *Indianapolis Star.*
But my father's deepest love was music.
He played the kettledrum, the snare drum, the celeste
in a small weekend orchestra.
Did my father know, when he tapped the celeste, that crystals
shattered in the ionosphere? Now my father's flesh is dust.

All of those machine guns and pistols like the stopped
crash of the cymbal; like the hard skin of the drum,
like something that was coming, that was merging; like the dust,
gathering and darkening in this spiral arm of the galaxy.

Song of the Mouse

As cereses,
as clue clocked
do diamond
dith array,
it cameith down
all gnarled,
clutched clothily
thouist go step
step under
smurl, snay,
wib nub
nosen out nest,
sub, sub, sub.

Translation: Snows light, but deeply, and a mouse goes under fallen branches to a dug-out soft placc… to the blind baby mice where she curls down to sucklc them.

Acrostic

Whatever good befalls us now,
after this pact, or whatever evil,
loosens the bloom upon the bough.
This way is marked forever double.
Ever shared in fine or coarse,
reckoned in pleasure or remorse.

So shall it be, the flesh is wed,
the spirit enters the marriage bed.
One chain or silken tie or kiss
nails the lovers upon their bliss.
Each is the food the other is fed.

Part the flesh, it shall not be severed.
Here is a joint defying time.
Drawn is the pact where the hearts endeavored.

The Möbius Strip of Grief

When I went into the room where you waited,
you said you were not staying here with me.
Angry, I went back to get an ice pick
where a large block of ice lay on the stairs.
It froze my fingers when I tried to lift it.
I am not a murderer, even in the brilliance
of sleep where poems are three-dimensional.
How often you come this way
in your cold contempt for my ignorance.

Where I Am

I'm not in a stone dungeon
under the streets of some Roman city.
I'm only in darkest Binghamton,
a second-floor apartment
in the company of two cats.
I have a plastic bag of dates
that claim to be grown naturally.
But how else can dates grow?
I see them hanging in huge clusters
from date palms,
as I once saw them from a bus
in the foothills of Southern California;
the streets of a small town,
adobes, lounging Indians,
a trading post. Then the fields of irrigation
and the forced water
spraying the great furrowed squares.
But I am here, not in a stone dungeon,
but in Dungeon Stone—
darkest Binghamton.

Weapons

My student's father
Embezzled the company,
His own,
And traveled. Went
To Swaziland,
Collected weapons.
She herself laughs
Hysterically, is
Obsessive about
Which university
To try next.
Her parents live
In the same house,
And while he was in
Mongolia on one of his
Impulsive trips
She and her mother
Hid her father's
Gun collection,
Some ninety or so
Exotic weapons,
In her mother's aunt's
Basement.
Still, the student
Who returned from three
Semesters in Germany,
To take creative writing here
On an impulse,
Feels that next year

She would like to expand,
Go work with the best writers,
Although she has only
Been into poetry
For the last six months.
She can still get financial backing
So she is submitting
Ten or eleven poems,
Surreal and wrenched
From her unconscious.
And what do I know
About creative writing?
This rapidly mutating world
Appears and disappears
Like the astrophysicists'
Description of subatomic
Particles blinking in
And out of the fabric
Of space and time.
Who am I to say, words,
Words, those tiny
Worms of sound,
Those strange firing puffs
Of disintegrating flesh;
This sack of
Self-propelling flesh that
For ninety-one years
Has been calling itself me.

Poetry

The sentence is basically a story.
Even a few words attach to the lifetime.
The mouth cannot forget
the story of the fingers.

Like comb jelly,
like canned condensed air,
like the full sac of the cobra;
the bitter milk of the tongue.

Bus Station

The toilets ooze like suppurating sores.
The resident homeless talks to herself.
Wearing all her worldly goods in layers;
her voice comes out of that cocoon.
She sits on tile floor against the damp wall,
holding two bulging trash bags.
She is having an animated conversation
with the empty room. Something angers
her. She argues. Then her head droops.
She dozes. She dozes as I do at night
in my bed, with the lamp in my eyes,
the phone on the bedside table, my glass
of water, aspirin, chocolate mints, emergency
numbers. As I do, snugged in my warm
blankets; a book, let's say, *The Best American*
whatever, slipping between my fingers.

This

This is the brown mud
This is the dry winter grass
This is the water of the sky
These are wet veins of the land
These are the rocks wearing smooth
These are standing factories of the air
These are the leaves
These are the starch into sugar
photon pinball machines
These are the breathers
This is the recycling ocean
This is the ozone layer

From the Porch

What is a wild tree
but the tops of the maples
when a storm
brawls up the mountain.
Or chokecherry smothering
the barn with its interlocking roots.
Or the entire mountain in September—
yellow and scarlet
and then turning brown
from the mountaintop,
slowly descending in front,
the dirt road
swirling past in a flutter of leaves.

What to Do

In someone else's house
you are not exactly at ease.
It's a matter of protocol.
That is, sequence.

There are unspoken rules.
Some of these rules are
under the rug—
so to speak.

You employ
a mechanical mouse
to investigate.

Progression

Now oaks, in progression,
hold their old leaves,
the same drab,
dun-colored
worn gold-plate of every field,
the color of Kansas winter
after a snow melt.

Now telephone poles,
linking the past with the future,
and elms,
thrusting their thinning crowns:
survivors,
like the retired farmers,
whose weathered faces
grow pale away from the fields.

These farmers, who ride the trains
to the sunbelt with their wives—
their busy wives,
carrying blankets to tuck in
the long skinny worn-out bodies,
grown tractable beside them.
Hawking and spitting, these men cough
from years of crop sprays and dust.

Now, from the train window
a dark road winds to a trim house.
The narrow severe farmhouses, repaired,

renewed after the Great Depression.
This land that we pass,
now sun, now shade,
and those square, white patches of snow,
that shine like large false teeth.

Kansas as Africa

The rolled hay is like hippopotami
and Kansas is the veldt.
The bare fields
after the snow is gone
pale gold in the sun;
and the occasional tree
twisted like the monkey puzzle tree
not yet leafed out,
dry and scaly.
And the blue snowmelt
makes water holes
for phantom zebras
and the slack stomachs of hunting lions,
in the gold grass gone to seed beside the tracks.

Wind Chimes

Glass wind chimes, and Aunt Kitty's
middle-upper-class house on the
north side of Indianapolis.
She kept a maid.
Aunt Kitty's husband, Uncle Colonel,
would say to me whenever
I came into his living room,
"Simmer down."
But I was only eight or so
and Mama had left me with Grandma
and gone to visit her mother in the South.
So there I was in Indianapolis.
After dark, wearing only a skimpy petticoat,
I would run through the sprinkler.
I loved my grandma and Aunt Kitty
but I missed my mother.
One evening Cousin Delores
and her boyfriend were on
the front porch swing.
I had asked my cousin Delores
not to tell her boyfriend
that I was wearing only a petticoat.
To my horror, I heard her tell him
and they both laughed.
I was stuck in the dark under the sprinkler
until Grandma came out with a towel
and took me up to bed.
I watched Grandma undress. She wore
many layers and under all, a corset.

Then she put on a long nightgown.
I lay beside her and listened
to the delicate clink
of the glass wind chimes
that hung in the open window.

Eve, Also

Holding in my left hand an apple;
they told me it was naturally grown.
No sprays. Or if sprayed,
the spray's not as deadly as some;
the skin, red as a Vermont
sunset in late summer,
when something, insects, pollution,
thickens the lower layers of air
and the light shifts to deep red,
slanting up from the rim of the world
that slopes downhill from us and then
the entire mountain and valley
are bathed in it.
As if the sun is a giant ruby—
a jewel like Betelgeuse.
All this while, I am eating the apple;
its insides glowing
like the summer sun that rises
at the edge of morning.
A crisp yellow-white,
full of miracles;
eating its moderately poisoned fruit,
in this careless moment,
in this careless moment of light.

The Fig Tree

Old as the world,
lithe and smooth,
her skin cool as a python's,
offers fat tongues of syrup
embedded with her seeds.
She gathers light for the tiny ones
through lobed waxed leaves,
the sheen of stoma,
the enzymic chlorophyll;
drawing up with her powerful veins
exact minerals for each cell.
How calm, like a lover waiting in the garden,
her pale trunk curving, sinuous,
dripping her raw smell in the carnal air.
She sways while a thousand beating wings
deflower her.

How It Is

The sensible living
aren't interested in the dead,
unless there is money in it.
So little you can do with them.
What they say is in your head.
They visit in dreams but turn their backs
when you beg them to stay.
They are never hiding in your closet.
Empty jackets, loose sleeves yawn
on the hangers. Their cold feet
that they rubbed and rubbed
with their long sensitive fingers,
before they put on their socks,
never come back with their fine
fitted bones to warm your bed.

The Dilemma

The eyes go outward
toward the Other.
The body remains hunched
in itself.
The generous eyes
caress the great
three-dimensional objects;
the body is the pumping station—
thump, thump.

The head, of course,
is the driver.
"My God," it says.
"I can't see where I am going."

Even Now

In the southern sky I hear there is
a catastrophic star—
Eta Carinae.
Perhaps it is so.
Around here the terrible event
was how Bush became president.

Of course, this Bush is no star.
No doubt as a major league
at the helm of the state
he will fade away—
meanwhile, Eta Carinae
waits in the wings.

No Doubt

No doubt you are a cup of coffee,
the anxious stomach murmured,
after a long night in the immaterial
arms of Wallace Stevens.
But are you real?
Perhaps I will digest this notebook
of blank pages.
If I were the eyes and the nose

it would be otherwise.

The Long Chill

The blankets scream to be folded.
After all it's almost noon;
the sun's pale powder glittering
and with no clear demarcation,
and too chill; as if when
the mammoths, strolling on the steppes
and consorting, paused, as usual;
as the first light dust of snow began to fall.

Goshen

For fifteen years I have lived in a house
without running water or furnace.
In and out the front door
with my buckets and armloads of wood.
This is the mountain.
This is the fortress of ice.
This is the stray cat skulking in the barn.
This is the barn with vacant windows
that lifts like a thin balsa kite
in the northeasters.
These are the winter birds
that wait in the bushes.
This is my measuring rod.
This is why I get up in the morning.
This is how I know where I am going.

Marcia

This distance between us
which stretches and shrinks,
as the breathing trees,
exhaling their oxygen,
lift and sigh with the weight of the world,
clasped by the molten center.

How in this braided pattern
we dance in and out
of our bodies which dance in and out
themselves, never one thing or the other.

What is this that we are
so like the mist that changes to water;
this rocking tide that we remember
imperfectly in our separate skins.

Burdened with ourselves,
as we love one another,
how to escape the unyielding law of the universe,
the self and the Other;
imperfect love.

That the self, sometimes
in sleep, admits the loss, the grief, and accepts
the burden of loneliness; embracing
what we will not admit we long for;
this separation of mother and daughter.

Where Is Everybody?

Everything brushes against everything
and hopes for a free ride.
Lisp, shudder,
fur on the cats,
patches of black and white,
under that, the mites,
then the pink-skinned forests of fungi.
Overhead the wind,
a layer of sagging crystals,
lets down rain.
Burdock pushes up,
stretches down,
making sticky bundles of seeds.
Seeds that silently snarl, "Touch me."
You move on, stuck with barbed clutches.
So where are the thistle eaters?
Their tiny bones glowing with DDT,
sucked into the soil long ago,
stretched out dead—
done in by Monsanto, etc.,
and their guaranteed weed-killers.

Old Cars

Old cars crouch like animals at bay.
They are the exhausted ocelots and tigers
out prowling. In them we were
sleek and long sinewed.
Speed was a given, even an imperative
In order to keep them with us
we fix on a useful part.
We think of the mechanics,
the interchangeable selves of ourselves.
The valves of the heart.
Yes, the body rushing into the long
white line of the divided dark.

Arizona

Huge bubbly rock noses
push out of the sand.
Indians shoving up
from ancient burials,
massive as Silurian reptiles.
A vast encampment of yucca
waits for them.
Cholla, greasewood,
the earth trembles,
wind like a herd of ponies galloping.

Straight from the Mouth of the Head Honcho, and I Quote

"We're looking forward to the time
when we'll simply say,
we're taking our genes
out of circulation.
I believe, and my wife will,
I'm sure, agree with me,
that many of these genes
are just not up to American
quality and will not produce
born-again Christians.
In order to get the economy
back on track, these genes
will have to undergo stringent
deregulation to meet the standards.
We feel the Right to Lifers'
demands for euthanasia
for all those unfit above the ages
of useful employment is our only
choice. In other words,
if you can't work, you're a bum.
America doesn't need any more bums."

Certainly Not

The man across the seat
would cause a farmer to look thoughtful.
There's so much meat.
It flabs under his polo shirt.
His right thigh,
in slate gray pants,
is huge, gorged.
If roasted
you could get slices,
enough for thirty or more
at dinner,
and his right hand,
resting at his crotch,
would fill a quart jar
as pig's knuckles,
tender and sweet.
The red sloping face,
with full double chin
attached ear to ear,
his young bristle mustache,
snubbed nose, his head
drooped in flushed sleep.
Poor thing, he says he sleeps around
because his wife is sick.
That's so considerate.
What's marriage
without its little ups and downs?
Up with students
down with gals.

Gals are past thirty-five
and try too hard.
While I am at the whetstone,
naming the cuts,
the wrapped quarters,
even the little coral of his brain
could be packaged.

Yes, What?

You don't want to dish up the facts.
Although, facts are always shaky—
fax this, fax that—
although they may travel forever
in the so-called ether;
like those lost Russian astronauts
staring ahead with frozen eyes.
Even if some distant system
thawed them out—
even if all time is instantaneous—
what can you say?

One Year I Lived in Earlysville, Virginia

In an old farmhouse in the middle of poor pastureland
I came to know the suffering of beef cattle. I was
teaching at the University of Virginia at Charlottesville,
taking the place of a poet who had gone to New York
for the year. The house was also the poet's and I lived
with his cats and his furniture and his books and his
sorrow. Sorrow was everywhere. The fat woodchuck
who lived under the back shed would sit at sundown
on her front stoop with her short arms folded almost
over her stomach and enjoy a rest from digging new
runways or eating the sparse grasses. And over on the
next parcel, the hound dogs would lift their crass
voices, yearning to track her down. For a while a
student shared the house with me. A strange
enterprising young woman who told me how she wrote
her term papers by going into the library and looking up
old thesis manuscripts and copying them. It was
ingenious and probably took more work than writing an
original. But she loved the power of taking what was
not hers. She also won an important poetry prize by
using her friend's letters, chopping the paragraphs into
likely sections. The last I heard of her she was waiting
tables somewhere. Her sadness was like the sadness
of secondhand automobile salesmen.
Near the house, beyond the black walnut trees, an old
family graveyard, surrounded by a quartz-stone wall
and mostly filled with women, children, and many
unnamed babies. The student also haunted second-
hand shops and I went with her once because I

needed a coat. I had discovered Virginia was in the temperate zone. I was sitting at the desk on the second floor under the tin roof, where when it rained, as it often did in the afternoon; the noise was deafening, the lightning striking the ground with an immense bolt of zigzag blue. And the secondhand coat was hanging downstairs on a hook beside the front door. I had recently looked at some old-fashioned postcards. The early twenties, I think, and scenes of some hotel with ladies in dresses that were just beginning to reach their lower calves; ladies who probably still kept their handkerchiefs in boxes and their gloves in bureau drawers. And here I was, living in someone else's life, grieving for the half-starved cattle and the young castrated bulls who would lose the herd and cry out in their terrible lost-mother voices. The coat was a rebuke and not at all a coat that I would have normally worn. I wore blue jeans most of the time and sweaters. But the university was old and mostly male and I was only a visitor so I tried to dress in an acceptable way. The coat created the poem. But I expect some of my Edwardian grandmother got in it. Those endless closets and halls in the brain where the unknown hides; that open for a moment and then close again. That is where the poems come from.

Lighter Than Air

The fat girl next door would give us a nickel
to walk to the old man's store
and get her an ice-cream cone,
vanilla, of course, the only flavor then.
On Powotan Avenue, Aunt Harriet and I would take
turns licking it all the way back.
It was hot that summer and we longed
to go to Virginia Beach and put our toes in the tide.
It rained every day and the James River swelled
up to our doorsteps.
Aunt Harriet and I wore tight rubber bathing caps
and long saggy bathing suits. How skinny we were.
She was nine and I was six. The lightning flashed
and we hid in the closet; the thunder crashed.
We had straight, bobbed hair and bangs.
Once a dirigible moved above the tops of the trees,
with little ladders dangling down, and we waved.

Barren

At long last, the sun,
without knowing it,
produces a man.
In Hong Kong, New York,
Algiers,
they like to play
the futures game.
We, who have no futures,
whet their appetites.
They are playing the world market,
while the sun eats itself.
The yellow lioness
eating the placenta.
She has given birth
to a hydrocephalic globe,
the only one that lived.
Its structured neurons,
misfiring,
damaging itself.
Strapped to gravity,
it sees no cause and effect.
It's unfit, yet
the idiot was water blue
and full of promise.
Without proper offspring,
she is running mad
in her dilemma,
screaming,

"I am without child,
except this beast
that blows itself apart."

For Abigail on Her Birthday

Although the weed tree
Is covered with ants
And even woodpeckers
Are getting their share,
Some delicious
Formic acid
Is lining the guts
Of all mentioned above.
And yet,
How curious.
The ants are ancient,
The birds are dinosaurs,
And I am an ape
Whose lineage
Is out-of-bounds.

Changes

The width of that road
changes as the honeysuckle bends,
as now in the rain.
The dark, not evening,
but the mountain's arm of clouds,
the sprawl of rivers of vapor.
For a while the planks of the house
will hold. Even as the front porch sags,
I cannot say stop. The rush outward,
like a daylily unfolding,
designed in the strings
of the mother lode, the stamens,
like the luna moth's wings
or the gonging of the sun's rising pulse,
from the deep center,
giving itself back to stasis.

Flowers

The pheromones of flowers;
old as the dinosaurs,
raptors that trembled the earth;
or those gauze fliers…
wings no human eyes beheld
and that strange anthropoid
that finally rose up from its knuckles.

Language

You can't move language.
It's like trying to take
a fulcrum to the world.
There's no base
to pry from.
It's that massy gravity.
If you try to pick it up,
it slithers through your fingers
like custard.
If you had time to reprogram
every cell of your brain,
you could go along
with language,
depositing the glacial loess
with white water leaking from it,
in flashing glittering veins,
spreading mineral moisture
ahead of its
crushing shapeless
groaning weight,
its crystal-locked phonemes.

Progression II

Let us,
or allow us,
or permit us,
or even urge us,
back us,
or underwrite us,
or collaborate with us,
or market us,
or copy us,
embroider us,
or create facsimiles of us,
or pour metal casts of us
for ultimate plastic molds of us,
for the deepest trash pits of us,
at the end of time for us.

Connections

What my eye sees
Goes into the dark
And passes, packet by packet
Along the ledge over the abyss
Between the lobes.
It goes so far
I think I cannot get it back
And when I least expect
Some of it returns
Not simple as it was
Or seemed
But now complex
And freighted with the universe.

In an Iridescent Time

1959

Memoir

Out of the shadows from the lamp at night we'd see
The lines of Braque on the walls,
Or where the shadow cut across the books, the free
Formality of a pink Matisse;
My eye recalls the mustache of Rousseau
Above my lover's smile,
The light delineates them so,
Each innocent of style.
Plaiting my hair the room would be at peace.

I recall him now, my lover of the academy,
How the page of my darling's ever-changing choice
Would be open to some unraveled evanescent verse,
As he grumbled on, a man alone with his voice.
Oh, not one word in an ordinary way
To tell us meanings reverse,
That the back of the hand is stranger
To the palm of the hand. Just the unmindful voice
Taking its single journey divorced from danger.

Out of the shadows of the street by day I see
The rain at the gutted curb,
Or where the fountains play in the circular masonry,
A verve without release,
The spew of a stone cherub.
My heart searches for some ingenuous grace,
And waits outside the room where all things cease.

The Magnet

I loved my lord, my black-haired lord, my young love
Thin faced, pointed like a fox,
And he, singing and sighing, with the bawdy went crying
Up the hounds, through thicket he leaped, through bramble,
And crossed the river on rocks.
And there alongside the sheep and among the ewes and lambs,
With terrible sleep he cunningly laid his hoax.

Ah fey, and ill-gotten, and wicked his tender heart,
Even as they with their bahs and their niggles, rumped up the thistle
      and bit
With their delicate teeth the flowers and the seeds and the leaf,
He leaped with a cry as coarse as the herders, "Come, I will start,
Come now, my pretties, and dance to the hunting horn and the slit
Of your throbbing throats, and make me a coat out of grief."
And they danced, he was fey, and they danced, and the coat they made
Turned all of an innocent mind, and a single love, into beasts afraid.

Was it I called him back? was it hunger? was it the world?
Not my tears, not those cries of the murdered, but 'twas the fox
Hid in the woods who called, and the smell of the fox, burned in
      his mind,
The fox in his den, smiling, around his red body his fine plume curled,
Out of the valley and across the river, leaving his sheep's hair, he left
      the maligned flocks,
I heard him coming through brambles, through narrow forests, I bid
      my nights unwind,
I bid my days turn back, I broke my windows, I unsealed my locks.

In an Iridescent Time

My mother, when young, scrubbed laundry in a tub,
She and her sisters on an old brick walk
Under the apple trees, sweet rub-a-dub.
The bees came round their heads, the wrens made talk.
Four young ladies each with a rainbow board
Honed their knuckles, wrung their wrists to red,
Tossed back their braids and wiped their aprons wet.
The Jersey calf beyond the back fence roared;
And all the soft day, swarms about their pet
Buzzed at his big brown eyes and bullish head.
Four times they rinsed, they said. Some things they starched,
Then shook them from the baskets two by two,
And pinned the fluttering intimacies of life
Between the lilac bushes and the yew:
Brown gingham, pink, and skirts of Alice blue.

The Season

I know what calls the Devil from the pits,
With a thief's fingers there he slouches and sits;
I've seen him passing on a frenzied mare,
Bitter eyed on her haunches out to stare;
He rides her cruel and he rides her easy.
Come along spring, come along sun, come along field daisy.

Smell the foxy babies, smell the hunting dog;
The shes have whelped, the cocks and hens have lost their wits;
And cry, "Why," cry the spring peepers, "Why," each little frog.
He rides her cruel and he rides her easy;
Come along spring, come along sun, come along field daisy.

In the Interstices

Pleasure me not, for love's pleasure drained me
Deep as the artesian well;
The pitiless blood-letter veined me.
Long grew the parasite before its fill.
Lover, smile the other way, nor ply me with evil
Who am surfeited and taste the shadows of gray;
Nor sway me with promises to rouse my thirst
And fill me with that passion beyond lust;
Nor romp my body in the wake of the mind's play.

How tired, how enervated, how becalmed I am.
That island toward which I strove in my salt tides
Has drifted out beyond the listless swell and formed
A hostile continent. I am amorphous with all deflowered brides,
Who, with their floodgates sundered, drowned when they were stormed.

The Burned Bridge

Sister was wedged beside the wicker basket,
Slats of hot midsummer striped her dress,
Speckled dust in shifting sun and shadow.
The trolley lurched to leeward, seemed to press
Our bodies backward in a flowered meadow,
Tossed Mama's brown hair sculptured in a puff.
Father rose and reeling from our side
Interviewed the trenchant motorman. How rough
The whitecaps glittered beyond the marsh;
Our pulses leaped at the stench of kelp and the harsh
Scream of the cormorant skimming the trolley wire.
Halfway on the clanging headlong ride
The trolley crossed a bridge charred black from fire
And reason impaled me, even through Mama's smile
And the arc of the motorman's tobacco juice.
"There, there," soothed Mama; "The deuce!" said Father.
But knowing better, I cried.
Though we went on for mile after summer mile
And arrived as we always did at the rank seaside,
All that held me up seemed wholly mad.
Not even the hidden drop-off, or bloated death
In the luminous choppy water, diverted my sad
Foreboding, or the derelict lighthouse in whose shade we lunched.
At sunset sister slept like a rosy anchor
Fastening parents to bench, and while they bunched
The tide rolled softly landward like her breath;
While I sat listening, wretched, without rancor,
Submissive on the bench beside the track.
Knowing, this time, the burned bridge would break,

I clearly saw my parents committed to folly.
Mama, for all her airs, could but clean and bake.
Now Father, as in a nightmare, would take us back;
And hooting around the bend came the feckless trolley.

The Awakening

Once when you turned to me and wound my hair
About my face, and in the dark your face
Was only a live felt thing, fear wrapped me too,
Disembodied arms held me in the bed's soft space.
Until you spoke, savagery crushed my throat,
And death like the snake slipped into our embrace.

Then by the light that later came cold
From the window, I saw you turned away
Asleep like a wax image, all of a color gray
And eyes shut down from all entwining, a fold
Of sheet between us, and my heart leaped up
To hear your voice, but your breath came easy, easy,
And your hands plucked aside my hair that brushed your face,
And there was a falling away from memory out of embrace.

Orchard

The mare roamed soft about the slope,
Her rump was like a dancing girl's.
Gentle beneath the apple trees
She pulled the grass and shook the flies.
Her forelocks hung in tawny curls;
She had a woman's limpid eyes,
A woman's patient stare that grieves.
And when she moved among the trees,
The dappled trees, her look was shy,
She hid her nakedness in leaves.
A delicate though weighted dance
She stepped while flocks of finches flew
From tree to tree and shot the leaves
With songs of golden twittering;
How admirable her tender stance.
And then the apple trees were new,
And she was new, and we were new,
And in the barns the stallions stamped
And shook the hills with trumpeting.

Home Movie

At the other end of a telescope, a long way,
There we are. How timidly you take my hand.
(Each seven years we have a whole new skin.)
Those lost creatures step back and back
Into a forest; under the virgin oaks they stand
And look about. All is dark leaves and the singular din
Of rubbing wings and repeated melodies.
(If we look at one another now the room will shake.
If we take our eyes from distances we crack.)

Now where following the call of birds will they step?
We might even smell the wood's mold and see mangled fern
Where they paused to embrace, where he touched her lip
With a delicate finger, wholly amazed at a boldness born.
(With our clay hands we hold to one another nor return
To the room which houses us, but sleep in a marvel of leaves
And sounds of wind shuttering leaves wherein our dead bodies mourn.)

The Mold

As you swing the door, your passage through air
sends back the pale vibration of your disapproval,
and crossly shakes the curtain, puffs the fire to flare,
and settles like coal dust, which though we remove all
signs of it with cloth and wax, is still there.

I would be with you on the ill-carpeted stairs,
climbing toward your unheated room in stretching pain,
that all-elastic anguish of the child. You think, who cares?
And following your tragic side up to the laceration of your prayers,
I recall the single beds where I have lain.

In this bruising of spirits and this pulling of feathers
from angel's wings, we reduce you to clay,
for that is how we are made. That airy flight in all weathers
subsides until, well formed, we drag from our beds toward day.

Swans

I

The swan she knew from many picture books.
It came in a cloud of snow
Settling light feathers on the lake.
And there was a goose girl quavering in the hedgerow;
An awkward goose girl henned and pecked.
And after a night of dreaming she would wake
To arms like sticks and legs like sticks, sacked
In a hand-me-down, and her heart would knock in the sun's fleck.
Many an orchard morning to the starling's creak
She turned her mirror to the wall and wept.

II

When Sal in time became the swan
It broke her heart to be ignored,
And from her proud beak hideously
Ignominy deplored.

Hissed at the corners of the house
And at the great maternal bed
Where in connubial hatred lay
Her soul disquieted.

When she was swan and light as air
It pleased her feathers to be flying,
And easily she let her tears
Dry in the wind if she were crying.

And she was swan upon the glass
And hid her long feet in the water,
And nipped the warm food-giving hands,
And sneered like the proper elder daughter.

Love's Relative

The couple who remain in bed
Are not alike; he's tanned and hairy,
Has a fierce Egyptian head,
She's dimpled, brief; alas, contrary.

Rather defenseless on the sheet
When morning oozes in the cracks,
Her tiny toes, his monster feet,
Both of them upon their backs.

Her years are two and his are thirty.
He's long and bony, somewhat glum.
Her little peaceful feet are dirty.
She sucks a firmly calloused thumb.

At some point in the evil dawning
This oedipal arrangement grew,
The leap from crib to bed while yawning
Mother in disdain withdrew.

O man, whose waking breeds confusion,
Protect the comfort of her sleep.
Hers is the primal bright illusion
From which she makes the bridal leap.

Vernal Equinox

Daughters, in the wind's boisterous roughing,
Pray the tickle's equal to the coat tearing,
And the wearing equal to the puffing,
As you match breath and tugging after the winter
In the thaw and the first heat of the sun's splinter.

In your first ramble, daughters, with your laughing
Loosed from the freeze when the grass is seeping,
Save your dimpled knees in the headstrong leaping.

And under his cloak, if you run with the north wind
When there is the smell of hibernation in him
And the black half-frozen waters of a dam,
Watch for his cruelty, he traps the lamb.

Daughters under the birches in the green weeping,
In the rain and lightning of the west wind's keeping,
Daughters, does, with tawny flanks shy stamping,
Nibble his water-quick land with your hoofs tamping,
And dance, do not rest, or he'll have you sleeping.

And daughters whose hearts are going
Higher, higher with your wild hair blowing
Into his high-riding giant's bellows,
Observe the tremble of the weeping willows.

FROM

Topography and Other Poems

1971

Dream of Light in the Shade

Now that I am married I spend
My hours thinking about my husband.
I wind myself about his shelter.
I watch his sleep, dreaming of how to defend
His inert form. At night
Leaning on my elbow I pretend
I am merely a lecherous friend.

And being the first to wake
Often wholly naked descend
To the dim first floor where the chairs
Hold the night before, and all says attend!
The light so coldly spells in innocence,
Attend! The cup is filled with light,
And on my skin the sun flashes
And fades as the shade trees bend.

The Talking Fish

My love's eyes are red as the sargasso
With lights behind the iris like a cephalopod's.
The weeds move slowly, November's diatoms
Stain the soft stagnant belly of the sea.
Mountains, atolls, coral reefs,
Do you desire me? Am I among the jellyfish of your griefs?
I comb my sorrows singing; any doomed sailor can hear
The rising and falling bell and begin to wish
For home. There is no choice among the voices
Of love. Even a carp sings.

Being Human,

Though all the force to hold the parts together
And service love reversed, turned negative,
Fountained in self-destroying flames
And rained ash in volcanic weather;
We are still here where you left us
With our own kind: unstable strangers
Trembling in the sound waves of meaningless
Eloquence. They say we live.
They say, as they rise on the horizon
And come toward us dividing and dividing,
That we must save; that we must solve; transcend
Cohesive and repelling flesh, protoplasm, particles, and survive.
I do not doubt we will; I do not doubt all things are possible,
Even that wildest hope that we may meet beyond the grave.

Tenacity

Can it be over so soon?
Why, only a day or so ago
You let me win at chess
While you felt my dress
Around the knees.
That room we went to
Sixty miles away—
Have those bus trips ended?
The willows turning by,
Drooping like patient beasts
Under their yellow hair
On the winter fields;
Crossing the snow streams—
Was it for the last time?
Going to meet you, I thought
I saw the embalmer standing there
On the ordinary dirty street
Of that gross and ordinary city
Which opened like a paper flower
At the ballet, at the art gallery,
In those dark booths drinking beer.
One night leaning in a stone doorway
I waited for the wrong person,
And when he came I noticed the dead
Blue color of his skin under the neon light,
And the odor of rubbish behind a subway shed.
I sit for hours at the window
Preparing a letter; you are coming toward me,

We are balanced like dancers in memory,
I feel your coat, I smell your clothes,
Your tobacco; you almost touch me.

The Excuse

Do they write poems when they have something to say,
Something to think about,
Rubbed from the world's hard rubbing in the excess of every day?
The summer I was twenty-four in San Francisco. You and I.
The whole summer seemed like a cable-car ride over the gold bay.
But once in a bistro, angry at one another,
We quarreled about a taxi fare. I doubt
That it was the fare we quarreled about,
But one excuse is as good as another
In the excess of passion, in the need to be worn away.

Do they know it is cleanness of skin, firmness of flesh that matters?
It is so difficult to look at the deprived, or smell their decay.
But now I am among them. I, too, am a leper, a warning.
I hold out my crippled fingers; my voice flatters
Everyone who comes this way. In the weeds of mourning,
Groaning and gnashing, I display
Myself in malodorous comic wrappings and tatters,
In the excess of passion, in the need to be worn away.

The Sun with Mr. Parker's Help

Mr. Parker scrubs the marble foyer Friday afternoon
With a string mop dipped in acrid antiseptic.
And he sighs at residents who shake keys out of leather bags
While they prop sacks of groceries on their hips and open the door
Trotting their withered spindles over his chessboard floor
Leaving tracks. His soft lips twitch, his cautious face,
Sculptured in amiability, contracts to scowl. He looks severely
At their backs. He falls to female crankiness, wringing his soggy rags;
And the elevator clanks to its own off-center tune.
But outside a hot layer of sunlight rots the slush.
The girl in number five careens out of her dark doorway, first floor end,
Her hair ready for wind, already across her face
Ready to whiplash like a mop out to dry on the line, all wild strings,
Followed by her weekend children dressed for the big day, the
　　　puffy rush
Of stout baby sitter, and glory to be, the mop-headed girl's boy friend,
Skinny pants, tweed jacket, and scarf about his neck, who flings
The outside door wide open herding them all out but letting in an
　　　old dog
Out of grace with its own feet, hobbling back from a walk in the sun
Ready to lie down in a warm spot. Mr. Parker leans on his mop.
A wind-lashed bush flickers light on the floor,
And only the clean glass door catches Mr. Parker's dissolving frown.

The Plan

I said to myself, do you have a plan?
And the answer was always, no, I have no plan.
Then I would say to myself, you must think of one.
But what happened went on, chaotic with necessary pain.
During the winter the dogs dug moles from their runs
And rolled them blind on the frozen road.
Then the crossbills left at the equinox.
All this time I tried to think of a plan,
Something to bring the points together.
I saw that we move in a circle
But I was wordless in the field.
The smell of green steamed, everything shoved,
But I folded my hands and sat on the rocks.
Here I am, I said, with my eyes.
When they have fallen like marbles from their sockets,
What will become of this? And then I remembered
That there were young moles in my mind's eye,
Whose pink bellies shaded to mauve plush,
Whose little dead snouts sparkled with crystals of frost;
And it came to me, the blind will be leading the blind.

Poles

In the summer under the light ease of laundry fluttering
In the air along with our portion of birds, insects and lifting leaves,
The simple truth is I confine your picture to one room
Where occasionally I go to be struck again by its fierce tragic stare.
Summoned to it by a world of trifles, in what I know is a mockery
Of despair; it depresses me. Though you cannot condemn or pardon
My being one with blood and oxygen, I damn myself
For having eyes and ears and wits, all the time I stand before you
Shaking my head at the shame of anything that lies down and dies.

Green Apples

In August we carried the old horsehair mattress
To the back porch
And slept with our children in a row.
The wind came up the mountain into the orchard
Telling me something;
Saying something urgent.
I was happy.
The green apples fell on the sloping roof
And rattled down.
The wind was shaking me all night long;
Shaking me in my sleep
Like a definition of love,
Saying, this is the moment,
Here, now.

Shades of Red

In the antique light of October, tiffany leaves.
Gamboge, buff, bronze and shades of red
Spread on the canvas of the gasping town;
New England's standing woodpile turned to heritage.
The local drunk clutching his bottle in a paper bag
Sits at one o'clock in the island of the park
To expose his old-fashioned humility
Under the vinaceous boughs.
For what does he exacerbate himself?
The radio gives the color of the foliage
And its degree of turning for those who travel north.
His gauge is not so much eccentricity as simple need.
Like the mushroom, whose main body is underground,
He bursts forth at intervals to admit his presence.
Across the way, watching the passing oil trucks,
Milk tankers, Ferraris, hairy cars,
They rest in rocking chairs on the porch of the Inn,
Having purchased little pillows of sachet,
Jars of ordinary herbs and maple-sugar candy
Shaped like soldiers in a box.
They hardly apprehend his modesty.
How can he know,
Sitting with the essential paper bag,
That he has local color like the maples
And turns with the season, unwittingly chemical;
Part of the windfall currency.

A Fowl Life

The churring leghorn has been chopped and bled,
Who was the quickest for the scattered bread.
The ax struck in the stump, her feathers
Float in the ruddy water. The young cock gathers
His ladies round him with an uneasy, faint
And faulty memory of his leghorn saint.
He takes them walking down the orchard row;
The wind lifts up the scattered down like summer snow.

Now whiten her with flour from the bin,
And light the fire and lay the lady in.

Birds

In Peabody Museum where Phoebe lagged and Marcia hid
Between the brass-cornered cases, we looked at the bird
That General Washington presented to his naturalist friend
In the city of Philadelphia. It had died of its own weakness;
And I forget whether it was a game bird of America
Or some exotic imported for his estate.
That we did not then know the two-volume work on the birds
Of Minnesota, or own a pair of binoculars, seems absurd
When I remember our eventual pursuit in the early mornings,
Field guide in hand, nothing at all in our pockets,
Trapped by circumstance on the Illinois prairie.
Then when the migration began, it seemed
As if thousands of yellow and gray birds beat in my breast.
Now when I am alone and I hear the vireo or warbler
Fluting the clear sound of time and timing,
I go to the brush where they are hid,
Trying to answer, here, here, I am here.

Breakfast in Paris with Nasturtiums

In the circle a marble fountain plays
Against the babble of the street,
Women meet on the way to vegetable stalls
And salad vendors humped under their braided baskets
Wheedle the sun-enchanted ear with their monotonous calls,
And sweetly, appropriately dressed,
A middle-aged lady takes her seat
At a round table in the shade
And looks at a bowl of nasturtiums.
The sidewalk is neat, the table is laid
With a clean cloth and floats upward in spice scent,
Whirls with yellow and red on stiff green stalks,
Almost tilting backward into a flowering hedge.
A gendarme, sleeping babies and an exploding Lambretta
Frame this delightful scene. The lady is complacent;
Soon she will be met by her more than middle-aged love
Who often presses her puffy fingers and fondles her name,
Henrietta, because he can do no more.
She prepares herself by removing a fresh white glove.
What is rare swings in the balance of timelessness
Like a shadowed door that opens upon the sun-drenched street.
Therefore the scent of nasturtiums and the fumes of the Lambretta,
The gendarme's whistle and the sleeping babies all wait with Henrietta.

Fairy Tales

The ugly duckling…
I stood behind my father's chair so he couldn't see my tears
When he read it to me. Hans Andersen,
I rise from your feathers every spring
And shake the snow out of my windows. The sulphur sears
My eyes in a world of match girls' luminous poverty.
I hear your hosannas that life is real and crucl.
The mad stream that takes the brave tin soldier down the flood
Flows by here. While he passes, impractical child,
On his way to death in this strange dream;
Is he still seeing the beautiful, the good?

Behind the Façade

My mother stayed in her small room
With the door not quite shut.
We watched TV in the living room,
Walter and I;
Secure,
Our arms lightly touching.
We couldn't remember
That my father had died.
Mother lay quietly
Staring into no language,
No touch,
The emptiness of nothing
Which had been there all the time
Behind the façade.
On the couch, with our backs to her door,
We leaned together
Talking about the children;
Our friends, the *Late Late Show.*
We felt our way among words
As on steel girders;
The structure multicolored, real.
Objects lay all around
Shaping the air.
Concrete as the glass of beer,
The cutlery;
Our arms holding one another;
Binding together what we said...
What we said... what we said.

Coda

Some thought about a shoe set me to stringing
The eyeholes of a memory. My mother, the old dear,
Would eschew such knowledge now for other than my ear,
But when she was a few months married, was in fact still singing,
She wore a pair of emeu-feathered slippers from the bed,
And dangled lazily about a little spangle house.
I suppose she spent time winding up her hair—it was then red—
And washed a few cups, the usual recess; I've seen a blouse
She wore in those days tucked to a formal stiffness, sweetly white.
How thin she was. The picture doesn't catch the tones
Of skin, the essence of her freshness, her light
Buoyancy. Now when she goes about with feathers
She wears them upon hats.
It seems so odd to me that once she owned a poodle
Who loved her silly shoes and took them up like bones
To chew and ate the feathers of long-dead emeus.
Because in all the time I lived with her she wore the plainest shoes
And all our pets were cats.

I Have Three Daughters

I have three daughters
Like greengage plums.
They sat all day
Sucking their thumbs.
And more's the pity,
They cried all day,
Why doesn't our mother's brown hair
Turn gray?

I have three daughters
Like three cherries.
They sat at the window
The boys to please.
And they couldn't wait
For their mother to grow old.
Why doesn't our mother's brown hair
Turn to snow?

I have three daughters
In the apple tree
Singing Mama send Daddy
With three young lovers
To take them away from me.

I have three daughters
Like greengage plums,
Sitting all day
And sighing all day
And sucking their thumbs;

Singing, Mama won't you fetch and carry,
And Daddy, won't you let us marry,
Singing, sprinkle snow down on Mama's hair
And lordy, give us our share.

A Mother Looks at Her Child

Why are you beautiful?
Was it your mother, your father,
Your genes?
I don't understand you.
Was it your aunts, your uncles?
I think of your unborn sisters and brothers,
Circuitous protein.
Who are they,
Lost in the serpent and the scale,
Who might have been?
Infinitely small
Ovoid, tail.
Why are you beautiful?

I am flesh set seal.
The other all.
Splitting skeins,
Roof, periphery, hall,
Doorway on the finite.
Why are you beautiful?

Are these the only eyes in which you flash
And flare in the burning blood?
There in the center, misunderstood
Great ornamental tree;
Limbs, sinewy arms, interlocking hair,
Igniting the air.
Separate flash whose fall cannot fail.
Why are you beautiful?

Changing

for Marcia

I like to write these lines to you
Because your eyes are green;
In between words there is a maze
I can't get through; a hedge
That might be holly, ancient holly
Clipped by men in rubber boots,
With wooden stiles hidden along the way.
But when I look at you again,
Your eyes are gray
And you have bleached your hair
And broken your heart;
But your brown hair is showing at the roots.
I think I'll climb a stile
And sit awhile
And listen to the blackbirds in the rain.
Love cannot be still;
Listen. It's folly and wisdom;
Come and share.

Tension

Anyone can say corn silk, field straw.
Girls with yellow hair are away—
Down the avenue in dresses
Like tents that the rain drew up.
They came out in the sun,
Taut to the rope, pulled by the boys.
Away—down the street, past the gray
Stained awning over the doughnut-shop
Window and far as the firehouse,
In dead-serious joy and worktime masks;
Planting their feet in the fertile heat
With the borer-nymph-grasshopper-
Root-knotter, summer-blowing wind in the street.

Advice

My hazard wouldn't be yours, not ever;
But every doom, like a hazelnut, comes down
To its own worm. So I am rocking here
Like any granny with her apron over her head
Saying, lordy me. It's my trouble.
There's nothing to be learned this way.
If I heard a girl crying help
I would go to save her;
But you hardly ever hear those words.
Dear children, you must try to say
Something when you are in need.
Don't confuse hunger with greed;
And don't wait until you are dead.

Healing

for Pheobe

Last night the children were here.
I went to bed before they left.
When I got up this morning
The house was brilliant;
Every light flashed its own sun;
Not a bulb burned out
But all sent ohms striking
The dust with the gaiety of headlong
Burning. And in the kitchen
The glorious remains of snacks
And little meals spread the color
Of tomatoes, onion peels;
The savory abandon
Of bodies heated.
All their energy lay about me
As I went in my pale gown
From lamp to lamp
Pulling the cords
And thinking
What delicious sleep I had;
I am not even sick any more.

Seat Belt Fastened?

Old Bill Pheasant won't trim his beard.
Weep, my daughters, and have you heard?
Sing, little otters; don't be afraid.
There's a rustle in the oak leaves
Down by the river. Oh, the moving mirror
And the hearer and the word.

Old Bill wandered in my waking dream,
A river dream; when I saw him come
I was riding by with my gas tank high
Down to Otter Creek from my just-right home.
And he put his beard in the window and said,
"It's sleazy and greasy but it's in your head.
Tell me, woman, do you carry a comb?"
Too far from home to the river, I shammed.
"Better not come this far," I said.
But old Bill Pheasant said he'd be damned.
And we backfired down. Oh, daughters, do you tread
On the leaf fall, fern all—picked and pocketed?

Now tell me when we're passing, and tell me when we gain.
And laugh, little children, while our gas tank's high.
"Give thanks for desire," was all he said.
"It'll either clear up or snow or rain."
So we tweaked his beard and we punched his head.
Is your seat belt fastened? Do you sleep in your bed?
If you're stuck in the river can you shift to red?
If you're coming are you going?
If you're living are you dead?

And we drove him away where the otters play,
Where it's twice on Sunday in the regular way,
Where they say what they know and they know what they say,
And the good time's coming on yesterday.

Fifteen

Today, angry and hurt, you ran away.
Not far; you sat under a sapling in the field,
A little darker than the grass matted around you.
Your long hair, your old fur coat
Shaded into the brittle calyxes:
Last summer's stems and flower heads
Dried into unyielding portraits of themselves,
Saying nothing but it is gone that was
In this too crowded air.

Hunger

I have been up and down the town
Looking for I don't know what.
The doors of houses are all shut.
Along the streets the hedges grow
Neatly between the houses, row
After row, all leafless now and brown.

What do I want, says eye to ear.
Whatever it is, it's guarded here;
Clipped and kept and the price is dear.
Are they all beautiful there inside?
Is what I want to be inside?

Past February and brilliant days
Burn pools of water in the snow.
Telltale visible breath and words;
Saw-toothed icicles crack their glaze;
I walk between the houses row after row
Pierced by the sounds of winter-crazed birds.

Metamorphosis

Now I am old, all I want to do is try;
But when I was young, if it wasn't easy I let it lie,
Learning through my pores instead,
And it did neither of us any good.

For now she is gone who slept away my life,
And I am ignorant who inherited,
Though the head has grown so lively that I laugh,
"Come look, come stomp, come listen to the drum."

I see more now than then; but she who had my eyes
Closed them in happiness, and wrapped the dark
In her arms and stole my life away,
Singing in dreams of what was sure to come.

I see it perfectly, except the beast
Fumbles and falters, until the others wince.
Everything shimmers and glitters and shakes with unbearable
    longing,
The dancers who cannot sleep, and the sleepers who cannot dance.

Wild Asters

I am here to worship the blue
asters along the brook;
not to carry pollen on my legs,
or rub strutted wings
in mindless sucking;
but to feel with my eyes
the loss of you and me,
not in the powdered mildew
that spreads from leaf to leaf,
but in the glorious absence of grief
to see what was not meant to be seen,
the clusters, the aggregate, the undenying multiplicity.

Topography

Do I dare to think that I alone am
The sum total of every night hand searching in the
Pounding pounding over the universe of veins, sweat,
Dust in the sheets with noses that got in the way?
Yes, I remember the turning and holding,
The heavy geography; but map me again, Columbus.

Cheap:

New Poems and Ballads

1975

Bargain

I was not ready for this world
Nor will I ever be.
But came an infant periled
By my mother sea,
And crying piteously.

Before my father's sword,
His heavy voice of thunder,
His cloud hung fiery eyes,
I ran, a living blunder.

After the hawker's cries,
Desiring to be shared
I hid among the flies.

Myself became the fruit and vendor.
I began to sing.
Mocking the caged birds
I made my offering.

"Sweet cream and curds...
Who will have me,
Who will have me?"
And close upon my words,
"I will," said poverty.

Cheap

Not knowing I wasn't free
I would slam the door
Of his rented hacienda.
He was young and cheap;
Sweet smelling sweat.
I was easy in my sleep;
Gathered my hair
In a simple plait;
Not fretting myself.
And surely as sun up
He would follow me
From century plant
To lemon tree,
Over succulents and thorns,
Down to the stretching sand,
To the naked hiss,
Where he'd catch my hand
And we'd run blind as moles
With supple skins
Rubbing together like skeins
Of trader's silk;
Braying, galloping
Like a pair of mules.

Sabbatical Love

Living in Selsey was like living in sin.
In the morning Mrs. Harmsworth came puffing
On her bicycle to tidy up. Dangerously red and purple,
Her veins. The wind in her.
The terrible story of her chilblains.
How you hated to give the gardener
His one pound six on Thursday
When he stood waiting at our door
With a wretched bouquet clipped from the mangy annuals,
"For her," waving it toward me.
How like the garden he was; those reproachful mounds
Of swollen marrows turning to slush,
The rich slime of the parsley bed.
Lover-like we sneaked away to walk on the shingle;
Leaving our neglected daughters in a playroom
Overlooking some faintly ominous shrubbery.
Were those puffins, gallinules, auks,
Crying around the muddy estuary? Where, in our middle-aged
      madness,
We climbed out over deep water
On piles and planks that had rotted in the continuous spray.

Codicil

I am still bitter about the last place we stayed.
The bed was really too small for both of us.
In that same rooming house
Walls were lined with filing cases,
Drawers of birds' eggs packed in cotton.
The landlady described them.
As widow of the ornithologist,
Actually he was a postal clerk,
She was proprietor of the remains.
Had accompanied him on his holidays
Collecting eggs. Yes,
He would send her up the tree
And when she faltered he would shout,
"Put it in your mouth. Put it in your mouth."
It was nasty, she said,
Closing a drawer with her knee.
Faintly blue, freckled, mauve, taupe,
Chalk white eggs.
As we turned the second flight of stairs
Toward a mattress unfit for two,
Her voice would echo up the well,
Something about an electric kettle
At the foot of our bed.
Eggs, eggs, eggs in secret muted shapes in my head;
Hundreds of unborn wizened eggs.
I think about them when I think of you.

Loss

I hid sometimes in the closet among my own clothes.
It was no use. The pain would wake me
Or like a needle it would stitch its way into my dreams.
Whenever I turned
I saw its eyes looking out of the eyes of strangers.
In the night I would walk from room to room slowly
Like an old person in a convalescent home.
I would stare at the cornices, the dull arrangements of furniture.
It all remained the same.
It was not even a painting.
It was objects in space without any aura. No meaning attached.
Their very existence was a burden to me.
And I would go back to my bed whimpering.

The Tree

I was a child when you married me,
A child I was when I married you.
But I was a regular mid-west child,
And you were a Jew.

My mother needled my father cold,
My father gambled his weekly gold,
And I stayed young in my mind, though old,
As your regular children do.

I didn't rah and I hardly raved.
I loved my pa while my mother slaved,
And it rubbed me raw how she scrimped and saved
When I was so new.

Then you took me in with your bony knees,
And it wasn't them that I wanted to please—
It was Jesus Christ that I had to squeeze;
Oh, glorious you.

Life in the dead sprang up in me,
I walked the waves of the salty sea,
I wept for my mother in Galilee,
My ardent Jew.

Love and touch and unity.
Parting and joining; the trinity
Was flesh, the mind and the will to be.
The world grew through me like a tree.

Flesh was the citadel but Rome
Was right as rain. From my humble home
I walked to the scaffold of pain, and the dome
Of heaven wept for her sensual son
Whom the Romans slew.

Vegetables I

In the vegetable department
The eggplants lay in bruised disorder;
Gleaming, almost black,
Their skins oiled and bitter;
A mutilated stem twisting
From each swollen purple body
Where it had hung pendulous
From the parent.
They were almost the size
Of human heads, decapitated.
A fingernail tearing the skin
Disclosed pith, green-white,
Utterly drained of blood.
Inside each skull, pulp;
Close packed, dry and coarse.
As though the fontanels
Had ossified too soon.
Some of these seemed to be smiling
In a shy embarrassed manner,
Jostling among themselves.

Vegetables II

Saturated in the room
The ravaged curry and white wine
Tilt on the sink.
Tomatoes in plastic bag
Send up odors of resentment,
Rotting quietly.
It is the cutting room, the kitchen,
Where I go like an addict
To eat of death.
The eggplant is silent.
We put our heads together.
You are so smooth and cool and purple,
I say. Which of us will it be?

Periphery

You are not wanted
I said to the older body
Who was listening near the cupboards.
But outside on the porch
They were all eating.
The body dared not
Put its fingers in its mouth.
Behave, I whispered,
You have a wart on your cheek
And everyone knows you drink.
But that's all right, I relented,
It isn't generally known
How clever you are.
I know you aren't appreciated.
The body hunted for something good to eat,
But the food had all been eaten by the others.
They laughed together carelessly outside the kitchen.
The body hid in the pantry near the refrigerator.
After a while it laughed, too.
It listened to all the jokes and it laughed.

Separate

I want to tell you something with my hands.
I have been weeding the garden.
Many young people come here
Playing drums, picking strings,
Holding their wooden hearts.
The radishes are strong and pithy;
The lettuce is bolting.
The leaves of the radishes are jagged like knives.
These young people encamp around their instruments
As though they are around a fire.
They watch for the signal.
It passes between them.
Sometimes I water the toads
Who wait for insects under the zucchini leaves.
Indian bedspreads are not as gorgeous
As the muted patterns of toads.
Sometimes I lift a green lacewing
Out of a trough of water
And it stretches up like a cloud
Filling the universe with a gauze torque.
I want to tell you something with my fingers.
The space between us is a crack in the ice
Where light filters green to blue
Deeper than the fissures of continents.
All of time stretched like a web between
Was sucked into that space.
I want to tell you something with my hands,
My enormous hands which lie across a broken mirror
Reflected in broken pieces of themselves.

As Now

In times of the most extreme symbols
The walls are very thin,
Almost transparent.
Space is accordion pleated;
Distance changes.
But also, the gut becomes one dimensional
And we starve.

Path

It was an old path.
It went uphill through the woods.
You led the way because you were the youngest.
"It's my path," you said.
Yes, these paths always belong to someone.
They crisscross through my mind,
The leaves smelling like campfire sweetness,
The dogs diverging in the underbrush.
But the woods; going up so straight and thin,
Leaves beginning to turn,
The shadows soothing, saying,
"Let us drift easy and lie down together.
Never go away, but lie here under this bush."

Communion

Birds circle above the hay barn.
A young bull gets up from the mud;
The tuft under his belly like a clump of grass.
He bellows; his curly throat stretched up,
His head half turned yearning upward from the wood slatted pen
Where he sleeps or tramples the sloughed manure.
The birds gather to cheep in unison.
A row of oak trees shining like waxed veneer
Ranges down wind-break.
The sky, vague blue behind a gauzy cumulus;
Pale fall sunlight glazes the barn shingles.
Now a chorus of bulls forcing music out of their bodies,
Begins and begins in terrible earnestness.
And the birds, undulating and rising, circle
And scatter over the fall plowed strips.
What they are saying is out of their separateness.
This is the way it is. This is the way it is.

Being a Woman

You can talk to yourself all you want to.
After all, you were the only one who ever heard
What you were saying. And even you forgot
Those brilliant flashes seen from afar, like Toledo
Brooding, burning up from the Moorish scimitar.

Sunk in umber, illuminated at the edges by fitful lightning,
You subside in the suburbs. Hidden in the shadow of hedges
You urge your dog to lift his leg on the neighbor's shrubs.

Soldiers are approaching. They are everywhere.
Behind the lamp-post the dog sends unknown messages
To the unknown. A sensible union of the senses.
The disengaged ego making its own patterns.
The voice of the urine saying this has washed away my salt,
My minerals. My kidneys bless you, defy you, invite you
To come out and yip with me in the schizophrenic night.

Cocks and Mares

Every man wants to be a stud.
His nature drives him.
Hanging between his legs
The heavy weight of scrotum.
He wants to bring forth God.
He wants God to come
Out of those common eggs.
But he can't tell his cock
From a rooster's. However,
I'm a horse, he says,
Prancing up and down.
What am I doing here
In the hen house?
Diddle you. Doodle doo.
In this fashion he goes on
Pretending that women are fowl
And that he is a stallion.
You can hear him crowing
When the wild mares
Come up out of the night fields
Whistling through their nostrils
In their rhythmic pounding,
In the sound of their deep breathing.

The Nose

Everyone complains about the nose.
If you notice, it is stuck to your face.
In the morning it will be red.
If you are a woman you can cover it with makeup.
If you are a man it means you had a good time last night.
Noses are phallic symbols.
So are fingers, monuments, trees, and cucumbers.
The familiar, "He knows his stuff," should be looked into.
There is big business in nose jobs,
The small nose having gained popularity during the Christian boom.
Noses get out of joint but a broken nose
Is never the same thing as a broken heart.
They say, "Bless your heart." "Shake hands." "Blow your nose."
When kissing there is apt to be a battle of wills
Over which side your nose will go on.
While a nose bleed, next to a good cry, is a natural physic;
A nosey person smells you out and looking down your nose
Will make you cross-eyed.
Although the nose is no longer used for rooting and shoving,
It still gets into some unlikely places.
The old sayings: He won by a nose, and,
He cut off his nose to spite his face,
Illustrate the value of the nose.
In conclusion, three out of four children
Are still equipped with noses at birth;
And the nose, more often than not,
Accompanies the body to its last resting place.

FROM

Second-Hand Coat:
Poems New and Selected

1987

Second-Hand Coat

I feel
in her pockets; she wore nice cotton gloves,
kept a handkerchief box, washed her undies,
ate at the Holiday Inn, had a basement freezer,
belonged to a bridge club.
I think when I wake in the morning
that I have turned into her.
She hangs in the hall downstairs,
a shadow with pulled threads.
I slip her over my arms, skin of a matron.
Where are you? I say to myself, to the orphaned body,
and her coat says,
Get your purse, have you got your keys?

Where I Came From

My father put me in my mother
but he didn't pick me out.
I am my own quick woman.
What drew him to my mother?
Beating his drumsticks
he thought—why not?
And he gave her an umbrella.
Their marriage was like that.
She hid ironically in her apron.
Sometimes she cried into the biscuit dough.
When she wanted to make a point
she would sing a hymn or an old song.
He was loose-footed. He couldn't be counted on
until his pockets were empty.
When he was home the kettle drums,
the snare drum, the celeste,
the triangle throbbed.
While he changed their heads,
the drum skins soaked in the bathtub.
Collapsed and wrinkled, they floated
like huge used condoms.

Poetry

I sit with my cup
to catch the crazy falling alphabet.
It crashes, it gravels down,
a fault in the hemispheres.
High-rise *L*'s, without windows—
buckling in slow motion;
Subway *G*'s, *Y*'s, twisted,
collapsing underground:
screams of passengers
buried in the terrible phonemes,
arms and legs paralyzed.
And no one, no one at all,
is sifting through the rubble.

How to Catch Aunt Harriette

Mary Cassatt has her in a striped dress with a
child on her lap, the child's foot in a wash basin.
Or Charlotte Mew speaks in her voice of the feeling
that comes at evening with home-cawing rooks.
Or Aunt Harriette sometimes makes an ineffable
gesture between the lines of Trollope.
In Indianapolis, together we rode the belching city bus to
high school. It was my first year, she was a senior. We were
nauseated every day by the fumes, by the unbearable
streets. Aunt Harriette was the last issue of my
Victorian grandparents. Once after school she
invited me to go with her to Verner's.
What was *Verner's?* I didn't ask and Aunt Harriette didn't say.
We walked three miles down manicured Meridian.
My heels rubbed to soft blisters. Entering an empty
wood-echoing room fronting the sidewalk,
we sat at a plain plank table and Aunt Harriette
ordered two glasses of iced ginger ale.
The varnish of light on Aunt Harriette
had the quality of a small eighteenth-century
Dutch painting. My tongue with all its buds intact
slipped in the amber sting. It was my first hint
of the connoisseur, an induction rarely repeated;
yet so bizarre, so beyond me,
that I planned my entire life from its indications.

What Can You Do?

Mrs. Dubosky pulls a handful
of sharpened pencils out of her apron pocket.
They're for the grandchildren.
She picks envelopes out of wastepaper baskets
and soaks off the stamps.
The boys have a stamp collection.
Mrs. Dubosky is paying on a trailer.
She can't retire until she's paid off the seven thousand.
She's sixty-two.
Mrs. Dubosky says, "We'll see."
Her new daughter-in-law lives in the trailer.
Her old daughter-in-law has the house.
"What are you going to do?" Mrs. Dubosky says,
looking at me. "He's my only son.
He'd come home. Want a kiss.
You know, those private things.
He's away all week pulling that semi to New Jersey.
And she says, 'Not now, I'm busy.'
Or, 'Leave me alone.'
He says, 'Ma, right then I knew.'
He made himself a bed upstairs.
He said, 'Let her go on, who cares?'
Then he asked her, 'How come Don is here
when I get home midnight? He's got a wife and kids.
What's he doing here all the time?' And she says,
'Are you accusing me?'
You know, I had my trailer on my son's land.
I had the hole under it for the flush toilet
and I had to move it to a trailer park.

That woman got everything."
Mrs. Dubosky wears other people's old tennis shoes.
Chemicals in the cleaning water eat right through them.
She's got a bad leg.
Her mother's legs were bad. They had to be amputated.
While her mother was in the hospital,
her father's colostomy quit working and he got a blockage.
Her mother told her, "You burnt him. I know you did."
"Oh, no, Ma."
"Yes, you did," she said. "I saw it in the paper."
"Marriage," says Mrs. Dubosky. "You know how it is.
I had just had the baby.
My husband was after me all the time.
You know, physical.
Oh, he slapped me but that's not what I mean.
My mother came over and she said,
'What's the matter with you?'
You know, the eyebags was down on the cheeks.
I says, 'He's always after me,'
and she says, 'You're gonna come home.'
The judge said he'd never seen a case that bad.
You know what he called him? He said,
'You're nothing but a beast.'"
Mrs. Dubosky isn't sure. She says,
"What can you do?"
When she retires, she tells me,
she's going to get a dog. One of those nice little ones.
"When you rub them on the belly
they lie back limp," she says, "and just let you."

Drought in the Lower Fields

Steers are dumb like angels,
moony-eyed, and soft-calling
like channel bells
to sound the abyss,
the drop-off in the fog
that crows circle
and gliding buzzards
yearn down into with their small
red heads bent
looking for dead souls to pick.
Steers nod their heads, yes,
browsing the scalded grass,
they eat around the scarce
blue stars of chicory.

Pokeberries

I started out in the Virginia mountains
with my grandma's pansy bed
and my Aunt Maud's dandelion wine.
We lived on greens and back-fat and biscuits.
My Aunt Maud scrubbed right through the linoleum.
My daddy was a Northerner who played drums
and chewed tobacco and gambled.
He married my mama on the rebound.
Who would want an ignorant hill girl with red hair?
They took a Pullman up to Indianapolis
and someone stole my daddy's wallet.
My whole life has been stained with pokeberries.
No man seemed right for me. I was awkward
until I found a good wood-burning stove.
There is no use asking what it means.
With my first piece of ready cash I bought my own
place in Vermont; kerosene lamps, dirt road.
I'm sticking here like a porcupine up a tree.
Like the one our neighbor shot. Its bones and skin
hung there for three years in the orchard.
No amount of knowledge can shake my grandma out of me;
or my Aunt Maud; or my mama, who didn't just bite an apple
with her big white teeth. She split it in two.

Liebeslied

The landlord's child
cries at night
in the next room.
It is early winter
and bright
in the morning,
the leaves of the apricot
still firmly attached.

Out by the oleander
a female cat
who lives wild
among these tract houses
waits for the food
I have begun to put outside.
Sometimes two half-grown
kittens come with her.

I look at the folded plastic chairs
thrown carelessly down
on the cement patio,
the toy truck
stopped in its forward surge
just where it is
loaded with mildewed walnuts.

I remember my father
whistling late at night.
He is walking along Irvington Avenue

from the streetcar line.
Alone, downstairs
he winds up the phonograph—
at the wavering edge
Fritz Kreisler's "Liebeslied."
I listen in the dark
to the bowed strings of sadness and pain
to what the human voice
beyond itself
is telling me.

Curtains

Putting up new curtains,
other windows intrude.
As though it is that first winter in Cambridge
when you and I had just moved in.
Now cold borscht alone in a bare kitchen.

What does it mean if I say this years later?

Listen, last night
I am on a crying jag
with my landlord, Mr. Tempesta.
I sneaked in two cats.
He screams, "No pets! No pets!"
I become my Aunt Virginia,
proud but weak in the head.
I remember Anna Magnani.
I throw a few books. I shout.
He wipes his eyes and opens his hands.
OK OK keep the dirty animals
but no nails in the walls.
We cry together.
I am so nervous, he says.

I want to dig you up and say, look,
it's like the time, remember,
when I ran into our living room naked
to get rid of that fire inspector.

See what you miss by being dead?

Winter

The ten o'clock train to New York,
coaches like loaves of bread powdered with snow.
Steam wheezes between the couplings.
Stripped to plywood, the station's cement standing room
imitates a Russian novel. It is now that I remember you.
Your profile becomes the carved handle of a letter knife.
Your heavy-lidded eyes slip under the seal of my widowhood.
It is another raw winter. Stray cats are suffering.
Starlings crowd the edges of chimneys.
It is a drab misery that urges me to remember you.
I think about the subjugation of women and horses;
brutal exposure; weather that forces, that strips.
In our time we met in ornate stations
arching up with nineteenth-century optimism.
I remember you running beside the train waving good-bye.
I can produce a facsimile of you standing
behind a column of polished oak to surprise me.
Am I going toward you or away from you on this train?
Discarded junk of other minds is strewn beside the tracks:
mounds of rusting wire, grotesque pop art of dead motors,
senile warehouses. The train passes a station;
fresh people standing on the platform,
their faces expecting something.
I feel their entire histories ravish me.

Shadows

I receive a card that says you have a walled garden,
a pomegranate tree. You sometimes go to Shiraz.
You have thrown a blanket over your table.
Underneath there is a lamp to warm your feet.
The maid, Batool, works all day long for a few rials.
Her son takes her money.
Her husband divorced her with three words.
You send a color photograph
in which your shadow crosses a bed of flowers.
There is a garden pool, espaliered grapes,
an orange and blue striped awning over a terrace.
"Along the street," you say, "the men hold hands.
The women are covered with black chadors."
You have gone to the mountains to ski.
You are in love. You have lost twenty pounds.
You chain smoke. You miss me. You need money.

The letter lags a month behind.
Your shadow sways with a donkey
stippled on Carpathian grass.
The rippling plateau fades toward the mountains of Iran.

I search for you in flashing neurons.
Across wrinkled dunes beyond hearing,
pure random donkey bells, dry resonance;
rocks sliding against the stubborn pull.
Mauve patches on the donkey's underbelly,
worn to smooth leather. Slap of thongs.
Below, falling away like the eye of God,
the deep iris of the Caspian Sea.

You May Ask

It is spring on the coast—
the sun behaving as it should
burning into the window
flashing against this poem.
This poem celebrates a fly
that softly rises above the desk.
Not arrogant, it thinks
where have I been? Where
am I now? What year is this?

Names

My grandmother's name was Nora Swan.
Old Aden Swan was her father. But who was her mother?
I don't know my great-grandmother's name.
I don't know how many children she bore.
Like rings of a tree the years of woman's fertility.
Who were my great-aunt Swans?
For every year a child; diphtheria, dropsy, typhoid.
Who can bother naming all those women churning butter,
leaning on scrub boards, holding to iron bedposts,
sweating in labor? My grandmother knew the names
of all the plants on the mountain. Those were the names
she spoke to me. Sorrel, lamb's ear, spleenwort, heal-all;
never go hungry, she said, when you can gather a pot of greens.
She had a finely drawn head under a smooth cap of hair
pulled back to a bun. Her deep-set eyes were quick to notice
in love and anger. Who are the women who nurtured her for me?
Who handed her in swaddling flannel to my great-grandmother's breast?
Who are the women who brought my great-grandmother tea
and straightened her bed? As anemone in midsummer, the air
cannot find them and Grandmother's been at rest for forty years.
In me are all the names I can remember—pennyroyal, boneset,
bedstraw, toadflax—from whom I did descend in perpetuity.

Why Kid Yourself

Snow, that white anesthesia, evaporates.
It's gone like a lover after the morning paper.
An entire mountain blushes.
Everything's been at it.
Embarrassing bodies are pushing out.
Plants, animals, swollen with excess,
are straining to keep their balance.
Two hot days and the population explodes off the circuits,
jams the sewers.
Afterbirth reeks in the swamps, gluts the rivers.
And everything that lived through last year
is out fattening itself, eating the babies.

Message from Your Toes

Even in the absence of light
there is light. Even in the least electron
there are photons.
So, in a larger sense you must consider your own toes.
Far from notice they spin
with their soft cheese-grains,
their ingrown nails;
your pink buds, identifying pads.
Down there the blood hurls
its collecting ooze of oxygen.
Down there the nerves thick as cables
in an ocean bed, collect barnacles;
clasped by octopods, send distant messages
years late, after the loved is gone,
the lips dead, after slugs have eaten
the remembered face. Relay how once
he stumbled across a room, breaking a bone,
a middle toe; how he suffered and couldn't wear shoes;
how his pain spoiled three months of summer.
How now, if you should dig him up, the bones of his left foot
falling like dice, there would be one among them gnarled out of shape,
a ridge of calcium extruding a pattern of unutterable anguish.
And your toes, passengers of the extreme
clustered on your dough-white body,
say how they miss his feet, the thin elegance of his ankles.

The Room

The room is the belly of the house.
It is pregnant with you.
It belches you out the door.
It sucks you in like a minnow.

You are a parasite in the room.
The room distorts with your ego.
It withholds itself from you.
It looks at you with criminal eyes.

Opinions insinuate from the baseboards.
The molding and ceiling are strange, erudite.
They see only the top of your head.
The floor, however, is continuously looking up your skirt.

The room keeps its weapons in a side pocket.
You should be hung in the closet, it says.
You should sweep up your hair, you are shedding.
You are spoiling my mattress.

Unable to hold your shape you dissolve in the room.
It fastens itself to your skin like a lamprey.
When you thrust yourself out the door,
it peels from your back and snaps like a rubber stocking.
It gathers itself in a corner and waits for you.

American Milk

Then the butter we put on our white bread
was colored with butter yellow, a cancerous dye,
and all the fourth grades were taken by streetcar
to the Dunky Company to see milk processed; milk bottles
riding on narrow metal cogs through little doors that flapped.
The sour damp smell of milky-wet cement floors:
we looked through great glass windows at the milk.
Before we were herded back to the streetcar line,
we were each given a half pint of milk in tiny
milk bottles with straws to suck it up. In this way
we gradually learned about our country.

How Aunt Maud Took to Being a Woman

A long hill sloped down to Aunt Maud's brick house.
You could climb an open stairway up the back
to a plank landing where she kept her crocks of wine.
I got sick on stolen angelfood cake and green wine
and slept in her feather bed for a week.
Nobody said a word. Aunt Maud just shifted
the bottles. Aunt's closets were all cedar lined.
She used the same pattern for her house dresses—
thirty years. Plain ugly, closets full of them,
you could generally find a new one cut and laid
out on her sewing machine. She preserved,
she canned. Her jars climbed the basement walls.
She was a vengeful housekeeper. She kept the blinds
pulled down in the parlor. Nobody really walked
on her hardwood floors. You lived in the kitchen.
Uncle Cal spent a lot of time on the back porch
waiting to be let in.

Comments of the Mild

The cabinet squats trembling on its carved legs,
an essence of trappings. Inside on the awkward shelves,
a cast-off bedspread, two stolen books.
From no period at all; in fact, the back legs are not carved,
while the front ones have turned balls. It tries to be Spanish,
Louis Quinze, Sheraton, Hilton Plaza. It is a bastard
from a tract house. There was no cabinetmaker.
It grew with a lot who were cut on band saws,
glued together on an assembly line, and stained
in a warehouse. "I am furniture," it says, in a subdued voice.
Not useful, not even ornamental, it has a certain bulk presence.
It takes the place of those who are not with you.
When you wake in the night, you sense that you are not alone.
There is someone else. But you forget who it is.
Sometimes passing the cabinet, you open the part that looks
like the confessionals box. It is stern and empty.
Nothing fits in there, not even your head.

When the Furnace Goes On in a California Tract House

If the blower is on
you may experience otherness—
then on the vinyl table
the clear plastic saltshaker
with her wide bottom, sexy waist,
and green plastic head,
her inner slope of free-running crystals,
is visibly crumbling
in the sight of the frankly opaque pepper
who seems taller, even threatening,
though they are the same size,
in fact, a designed pair.
His contents are hotter.
"Yes," she sighs, "the pepper is strong.
How he asserts himself on the cream soup—"
Or, "What is an egg without his gesture?"
Little does she suspect in her ability to dissolve
without losing herself, that the very blood…
"It's degrading," she confides, "the way they pinch me."

Surviving in Earlysville with a Broken Window

Mr. Garvey tells me old window glass is frail.
A man dealing in cattle has use of his fields, steers graze his worn
      out acres.
He lives in Charlottesville, receives my rent by mail.

He's in heating and plumbing. He acquired this property at a
      delinquent taxes sale.
A scrubby graveyard in the pasture, enclosed with clay and quartz
      walls, designates some earlier forsakers.
Mr. Garvey tells me old window glass is frail.

It rains on the metal roof. The young steers bellow. My pale
sticky letters are all bills that come late in the afternoon from
      moneymakers.
And if the university doesn't screw up, he receives my rent by mail.

I'm vegetarian, talk to the steers. I say we must love each other and
      the great blue whale
and the gone silly dodo who helpfully scored in its gizzard the thick
      endocarps of the, for all purposes now, extinct calvaria tree;
      coevolution of seed and seed breaker.
Mr. Garvey, who never fixes anything, tells me old window glass is frail.

The graveyard has headstones with names and weathered head- and
      footstones without names. I inhale
a sourmash smell of fallen pears hollowed out by bees, those
      indigenous sweet-rakers.
The cattle dealer is starving the cattle while Mr. Garvey receives my
      rent by mail.

The house inside has wooden walls; is simple, spare, even severe;
        handhewn board, each nail
hand cut, driven across the grain. It's drafty, hard to heat in winter,
        and remains an anachronism to the easy takers.
The steers cross the dry stubble like wound-up toys. They come to
        the fence at night and wait. Mr. Garvey tells me old window
        glass is frail.
He lives in Charlottesville, receives my rent by mail.

Happiness

We were married near the base,
with three days' leave;
a wife's allotment, a widow's pension.
The first night in our rented basement room,
as we came together...
Port Chicago exploded!
Several thousand pounds of human flesh
shot like hamburger through the air;
making military funerals, even with wax,
even with closed caskets, bizarre.
As well as certain facts:
there were no white males
loading ammunition on that ship.
From twenty miles away
shock waves rattled the roof,
the walls, the windows.
Our bed danced on the floor
as if we had created a miracle.

Then you went with your unit
in a leaky Liberty Ship to Kiska.
There in the shadow of a Russian church,
you began to notice birds.
One day you followed a snowbird over the tundra.
You followed it beyond sight of the camp, of the others,
as if for a moment there was a choice.
You felt a kind of happiness.
Your letters which told me this, with certain lines
removed, stamped out, sealed by the censor,

have been lost for years.
As the bird, filaments burning in a web of moss,
its tiny skeleton, its skull
that searched ahead of you like radar.

Turn Your Eyes Away

The gendarme came
to tell me you had hung yourself
on the door of a rented room
like an overcoat
like a bathrobe
hung from a hook;
when they forced the door open
your feet pushed against the floor.
Inside your skull
there was no room for us,
your circuits forgot me.
Even in Paris where we never were
I wait for you
knowing you will not come.
I remember your eyes as if I were
someone you had never seen,
a slight frown between your brows
considering me.
How could I have guessed
the plain-spoken stranger in your face,
your body, tagged in a drawer,
attached to nothing, incurious.
My sister, my spouse, you said,
in a place on the other side of the earth
where we lay in a single bed
unable to pull apart
breathing into each other,
the Gideon Bible open to the Song of Songs,
the rush of the El-train

jarring the window.
As if needles were stuck
in the pleasure zones of our brains,
we repeated everything
over and over and over.

Some Things You'll Need to Know Before You Join the Union

I

At the poetry factory
body poems are writhing and bleeding.
An angry mob of women
is lined up at the back door
hoping for jobs.
Today at the poetry factory
they are driving needles through the poems.
Everyone's excited.
Mr. Po-Biz himself comes in from the front office.
He clenches his teeth.
"Anymore wildcat aborting out there," he hisses
"and you're all blacklisted."
The mob jeers.

II

The antiwar and human rights poems
are processed in the white room.
Everyone in there wears sterile gauze.
These poems go for a lot.
No one wants to mess up.
There's expensive equipment involved.
The workers have to be heavy,
very heavy.
These poems are packaged in cement.
You frequently hear them drop with a dull thud.

III

Poems are being shipped out
by freight car.
Headed up the ramp
they can't turn back.
They push each other along.
They will go to the packinghouses.
The slaughter will be terrible,
an inevitable end of overproduction,
the poetry factory's GNP.
Their shelf life will be brief.

IV

They're stuffing at the poetry factory today.
They're jamming in images
saturated with *as* and *like*.
Lines are being stuffed to their limits.
If a line by chance explodes,
there's a great cheer.
However, most of them don't explode.
Most of them lie down and groan.

V

In the poetry factory
it's very hot.
The bellows are going,
the pressure is building up.
Young poems are being rolled out
ready to be cut.
Whistles are blowing.
Jive is rocking.

Barrels of thin words line the walls.
Fat words like links of sausages
hang on belts.
Floor walkers and straw bosses
take a coffee break.
Only the nervous apprentice
is anywhere near the machines
when a large poem
seems about to come off the assembly line.
"This is it," the apprentice shouts.
"Get my promotion ready!
APR, the quarterlies,
a chapbook, NEA,
a creative writing chair,
the poetry circuit, Yaddo!"
Inside the ambulance
as it drives away
he is still shouting,
"I'll grow a beard,
become an alcoholic,
consider suicide."

Women Laughing

Laughter from women gathers like reeds in the river.
A silence of light below their rhythm glazes the water.
They are on a rim of silence looking into the river.
Their laughter traces the water as kingfishers dipping
circles within circles set the reeds clicking;
and an upward rush of herons lifts out of the nests of laughter,
their long stick-legs dangling, herons, rising out of the river.

Translations

Forty-five years ago, Alexander Mehielovitch Touritzen, son of a White Russian owner of a silk stocking factory in Constantinople, we rumpled your rooming-house bed, sneaked past your landlady and turned your plaster Madonna to the wall. Are you out there, short vulgar civil-engineer? Did you know I left you for a Princeton geologist who called me *girlie*? Ten years later he was still in the midwest when he died under a rock fall. I told you I was pregnant. You gave me money for the abortion. I lied to you. I needed clothes to go out with the geologist. You called me *Kouschka*, little cat. Sometimes I stopped by the civil-engineering library where you sat with other foreign students. You were embarrassed; my husband might catch you. He was in the chemistry lab with his Bunsen burner boiling water for tea. Alexander Mehielovitch Touritzen, fig of my pallid college days, plum of my head, did the silk stocking factory go up in flames? Did the German fox jump out of the desert's sleeve and gobble your father up? Are you dead?

Second-hand engine, formula concrete, we were still meeting in stairwells when the best chess player in Champaign-Urbana went to the Spanish Civil War. He couldn't resist heroic gestures. For years I was haunted by the woman who smashed her starving infant against the Spanish wall. Cautious, staid Mehielovitch, so quick to pick my hairpins out of your bed.
Average lover, have your balls decayed?

Mehielovitch, my husband the chemist with light eyes and big head, the one whose body I hated, came back in the flesh fifteen years ago. He was wearing a tight western shirt he had made himself. (There wasn't anything he couldn't do.) He talked about wine- and cheese-tasting parties.

We folk-danced at a ski lodge. So this is life, I said.

He told my daughter he was her daddy. It wasn't true.

You are all so boring. My friend from Japan, Cana Maeda, the scholar of classical haiku, whose fingers, whose entire body had been trained to comply: her face pale without powder, her neck so easily bent, after she died from the radiation her translations of Bashō were published by interested men who failed to print her correct name. So the narrow book appears to have been written by a man. Faded in these ways, she is burned on my flesh as kimonos were burned on the flesh of women in the gamma rays of Hiroshima. She wasn't one of those whose skin peeled in the holocaust, whose bones cracked. Graceful and obscure, she was among all those others who died later. Where are you, my repulsive White Russian? Are you also lost?

Pimpled obscene boy employed at an early age by your father, you pandered his merchandise on trays using your arm as a woman's leg slipped inside a silk stocking with a woman's shoe on your hand. Do you understand that later I lived with a transvestite, a hairdresser who wore wigs? When he felt that way he would go out and pick up an English professor. After we quarreled, I cut up his foam-rubber falsies. I had a garage sale while he was out of town. I sold his mail-order high heels, his corsets, his sequined evening gowns.

Those afternoons in bed listening to your memories of prostitutes with big breasts, how you wanted to roll on a mattress of mammary glands; the same when Rip Hanson told me about the invasion of France. Crossing the channel he saw infantry, falling past him from split-open cargo planes, still clinging to tanks and bulldozers. Statistical losses figured in advance. The ripped-open

remnants of a Russian girl nailed up by the Germans outside her vil-
lage, also ancient, indigenous.
But what can I tell you about death? Even your sainted mother's soft
        dough body: her flour-dusted breasts
by now are slime paths of microorganisms.
Where were you when they fed the multitudes to the ovens?
Old fetid fisheyes, did they roll you in at the cannery?
Did you build their bridges or blow them up?
Are you burned to powder? Were you mortarized?
Did you die in a ditch, Mehielovitch? Are you exorcised?

Poor innocent lecher, you believed in sin.
I see you rising with the angels, thin forgotten dirty-fingered son
of a silk stocking factory owner in Constantinople,
may you be exonerated. May you be forgiven.
May you be a wax taper in paradise,
Alexander Mehielovitch Touritzen.

Who Is the Widow's Muse?

1991

All Time Is Past Time

Goliath is struck by the stone.
The stone turns into a bird.
The bird sings in her window.
Time is absurd. It flows backward.
It is married to the word.

This is the window of the giant's eyes.
This is the bird singing alone.
This is the river of forgetting.
This is the chosen stone.
This is Goliath's widow.

Struck by the stone he leaps
into the future. He lies
a monolith, a rune, light
from a distant nova. Not even a bone
remembers begetting him ever.

The song is a monotone.
She is the word and the window.
She is the stone and the bird.
She is the bed of the river.

I

Crow, are you the widow's muse?
You wear the weeds.
Her answer, a caw.
Her black beads:
two jet eyes.
A stick fire
and a thorn for her body.
Into the wind, her black shawl.

II

Sedated, tranquilized,
the widow is cut loose.
She rises in a basket
attached to a multicolored balloon.
It hauls her up,
her little casket,
into black blue frenzied gas molecules.
Below, her miniature house,
her small heavy car,
fixed on a square of grass,
disappear.

X

Hidden toward the back,
the widow tries
to feel part of a larger thing.
If asked,
she is quick to agree.
Never mind
if you can shoot a bean
through one of her ears
and have it come out the other.
She pretends she is a manikin
in a department store window.
See and be seen,
is her motto.
Perhaps the widow's muse
is her dead mother.

XIII

Alone in the car,
the widow makes songs to him.
She tells him her secrets.
The body of the car holds her;
it is not silent,
it too sings and responds.
She wonders if the muse is the car.
She and the car have
sculptured a comfortable place.
Her feet are at home.
Her hands clasp the steering wheel.
Her eyes seek the way
and the car knows.
Then why has she named the car
Violet Hunt?
The widow sighs. Here it is again—
gender and sorrow.

XVI

The widow has, unfortunately,
grown curious and is reading
The Egyptian Book of the Dead.
(Modern edition.)
It makes her nervous to think
of all those women
drinking poison
and lying down in the chamber
outside the sealed room
where the Pharaoh's body,
a resinous shell, packed
with oils and perfumes,
and wrapped in oil-soaked cloths,
is all prepared for their journey.
But then,
she was nervous when
she bought that double plot.
"Oh, if only
he hadn't done this,"
she says.

XVIII

I must be serious, the widow thinks,
I must face reality.
This isn't a temporary separation.
(Perhaps the widow's muse is expectation.)
Actually the widow thinks he may be
in another country in disguise—
that one day he will come back.
He was only fooling.
That was someone else that they buried.

XIX

Is the widow's muse
all the women of the world?
The widow runs her hands
over their faces,
like braille.
She reads them with her palms.
How complex they are.
They are as rich as sea broth.
Their minerals sparkle in the air.
"We sift through time
like the diatoms," she says,
"we multiply and add to ourselves.
Ai-yi, ai-yi!"

XX
The Widow's Song

As I was a springbok,
I am a leper.
As my skirt lifted up as a veil,
so the shawl of a widow.
As the oxlip,
so the buffalo grass.
As the wall of a garden in winter,
so was I, hidden.
As the game of the keeper...
not counted.
So I am without number.
As the yellow star grass.

XXI

The widow likes to wash sheets
and hang them on the line.
They are definite areas,
flexible squares,
tangible comfort.
The wind plays with them.
The widow likes to wrestle with
the body of sheets.
As she subdues them to
folded compact units,
and stores them in the linen closet,
she feels the muse may
dwell in the linen closet.

XXIX

The widow likes to ride on trains.
Trains are phallic symbols.
The engineer is probably on crack.
His speed outruns the antiquated equipment.
These trains were built for middle-aged engineers.
Once she and her husband
were fooling around on a train.
They were trying to torment
four old men playing cards.
The men's eyes were heavy lidded.
They looked at their hands.
Could the widow's muse be carnal?
Could she have hot pants?

XXXIV

The sun is coming through the ice patterns
on the window.
The widow is home.
She takes a picture of her dog
on the worn-out Persian carpet.
All night the widow dreamed of houses
and who owned them.
A deep sense of enclosure
comes over the widow.
"I will never be ignorant again,"
she says.
The muse lifts her eyebrow.
"Illuminations, final statements,
nutshells," the muse cries…
"blather, blather, blather!"

XXXVII

The widow thinks about the photograph
of toothless Maude Gonne
standing outside a polling booth.
How shameless she is,
tall and thin,
that political skeleton;
that lover of military men.
And the widow knows
that for a temporary time
Maude Gonne was the muse
of William Butler Yeats,
that Maude Gonne was Ireland.
And the widow McBride...
who was her muse?
Who was the muse
of all that flesh
gone to waste?

XLII

After thirty years
the widow gets smug.
"Well, I did it,"
she brags,
"with my own bare hands."
The muse shrugs.
"Uh-huh…
Did what?"
The muse leads her to
a back stairway.
There is his undershirt
in an old trunk.
"Smell that," the muse says.
The widow inhales his lost perspiration.
"You brute," she whimpers.
The muse takes a bone
out of her arm
and knocks the widow senseless.
"She'll never learn,"
the muse simpers.

XLIII

The widow wonders if she
is here on false pretenses.
Is this really her home?
After all, if he saw her now,
would he marry her?
The widow pinches the fat
on her abdomen.
There is dust on all the furniture.
Her fingernails are not clean.
The muse has deserted her.
"If you are not good enough
for him," the muse says,
"why should you be
good enough for me?"

XLIV

The widow looks at spring catalogues.
She feels a need to dig in the garden;
to eat, in the summer, the large
male flowers of the squash,
the ones that will not bear fruit.
She longs for stuffed squash blossoms.
This symbolic cannibalism
is a negative resurrection,
a logical illogic.
She allows herself in a dream
to lie along the ground
under a canopy of three-foot-
long green beans.
The muse is on vacation.
The widow gets a card from the muse.
"Am playing tennis every day with
Don Hall, Don Justice, Don Juan."

XLV

The widow puts on her Long Beach
Literary Women's Festival shirt.
Stained with coffee, it keeps
her company in bed.
That's where we wear our scars
and badges, anyway, she says.
The widow's muse was at the Festival, too.
She was that one with iron gray hair
and the large manila envelope of poems,
who sat next to the widow at dinner.
"Don't read those scary poems," the widow
said. "There are five hundred women here,
and they know all that.
Just get up and give them the old soft-shoe."

L

The widow accumulates meaningful trash.
She is no different from all the others.
"I should set aside a room for a shrine.
And how am I going to throw away their little toys?"
She joins the long line of sentimental mothers
waiting for phone calls.
Increasingly, the widow enjoys her grandchildren.
Sometimes she pauses to tell her dead husband...
"It's that time of life when we
should be taking a cruise; going to Europe;
going to Australia. But it's just as well.
The grandchildren need me.
You would have liked them, too."
The muse yawns. The muse is irritable.
"Yes, yes," the muse says;
"So what else is new?"

LI

It is Easter.
The widow wakes up to rain
on the roof. The basement is flooded.
The furnace is out.
"The only thing that is risen here
is the water," she says to herself.
"Once I was an egg.
A soft vulnerable X.
Possibly capable of parthenogenesis.
Then I was penetrated
by a renegade Y.
Then I developed into this...
a widow. But before then,
I wasn't a widow.
Before then I was a sun
lighting up the dark descent
into the fallopian tube.
I was autonomous.
I had come from forever."
"What a lot of drivel you are
talking," says the muse.
"Just quit it... which
came first, the chicken or the egg?"
The widow looked thoughtful.
"Actually," the widow says,
"I think it was the rabbit."

LII

The widow is told by a great seer
that fifty-two is a magic number.
She consults the muse.
"We must get into a higher gear,"
the muse whispers. "We must shift
out of this phase."
"Just one more about shoes,"
the widow begs.
The muse shakes her head.
"No. We must get back to the real thing.
The blood and meat of the world."
The muse took the widow in her arms.
"Now say it with me," the muse said.
"Once and for all... he is forever dead."

Simplicity

1995

Against Loss

That time at the Down Beat: Billie Holiday.
Oh, nothing is succulent and sweet anymore.
We drank so much.
This was before the war, when we
were renting rooms for the weekends;
and you watched me brush my hair,
tickling your long fingers down my back.
I sometimes hear the trombone and sax and drums,
the wobble of spinning glass above the Ladies' Room,
where she was up-ending a little toss
of medicine out of a bottle.
I mean, Billie Holiday spoke to me down there.
She said, "I've got a bad cough," like an
apology. And I remember her.
Memory becomes the exercise against loss.
Later, when we were naked on the bed,
and that tremble of heat lightning along the muscles,
you began the slow measures of "Dover Beach"
in the only voice—the only voice—
"Ah, love, let us be true to one another."

Ripple Effect

You don't want to hate this world.
The tassels of corn don't.
Even though they've been forced into slavery
they never think of their heads chopped off,
only of turning into starch.
Sugar into starch
is what they think.
And to think is to do.
Of course growing together has a ripple effect.
A field of corn repeats everything it hears.
"I ear what you say,"
says one stalk of corn to another.

Plumbing

Plumbing is so intimate.
He hooks up your toilet.
He places a wax ring
under the vitreous seat
where your shit will go.
You are grateful to him.
He is a god with wrenches;
a quiet young man
using a flame torch.
He solders the joints.
He crawls through your dusty attic
over the boxes of doll furniture,
the trains, the ripped
sleeping bags, the Beatles posters,
the camp cots, the dishes, the bed springs,
to wire up the hot water tank.
And you admire him
as you would Saint Francis,
for his simple acceptance
of how things are.
And the water comes like a miracle.
Each time in the night
with your bladder full,
you rise from the bed.
And instead of the awful stench
of the day before and perhaps
even the day before that,
in a moment of pure joy
you smell nothing but the sweet

mold of an old house
and your own urine as it sloshes
down with the flush.
And you feel comfortable, taken care of,
like some rich Roman matron
who had just been loved by a boy.

That Winter

In Chicago, near the lake, on the North Shore
your shotgun apartment has a sun room
where you indulge in a cheap
chaise longue—
and read *Of Human Bondage*—
There is a window in the living-room proper
cracked open so your
Persian cat can go outside.
You are on the first floor and upstairs
a loud-mouthed Southern woman,
whose husband is away
all week on business trips,
has brought her maid
up from Georgia
to do the work and take care of the baby.
"O Lord," the Southern woman says,
"he wants it spotless on the weekend—"
The maid, who has
smooth brown skin,
is not allowed to sit on the toilet
but she feeds the kid
and changes the dirty diapers.
She washes the dishes,
she cooks the Southern meals,
she irons the sheets for the mahogany bed.
The Southern woman shouts
at her in a Southern drawl,
"Junie, don't sit on that chair
you'll bust it."

The Southern woman is at
loose ends five days
waiting for him to come in.
"It's like a honeymoon,
honey," she says—
"When he grabs me,
whooee."
She invites you up and makes
sure you understand
the fine points of being a white woman.
"I can't let her live
here—not in Chicago.
I made her go out
and get herself a room.
She's seventeen.
She bellered and blubbered.
Now I don't know
what she's trackin' in
from men."
It is winter. The ice
stacks up around the
retaining wall—
the lake slaps over
the park benches,
blocks of ice green with algae.
You are getting your mail secretly at a postal box
because your lover is in the Aleutians.
It's during the war and
your disgusting husband
works at an oil refinery
on the South Side.
Up there in the Aleutians
they are knocking the gold

teeth out of the dead Japanese.
One construction worker
has a skin bag with fifty
gold-filled teeth.
He pours them out at
night in his Quonset hut.
He brags about bashing their faces in.
One day you are fooling
around in a downtown music store
waiting for the war to end.
You let a strange teenage boy
talk you into going
home with him.
He lives alone in a basement behind a
square of buildings.
He shows you his knife collection
and talks obsessively about Raskolnikov—suddenly
your genes want to live
and you pull away
and get out of there.
It is almost dusk.
You run until you find the boulevard
sluggish with the 1943 traffic.
You know by now there
isn't much to live for
except to spite Hitler—
The war is so lurid
that everything else is dull.

Resonance

The universe is sad.
I heard it when Artur Rubinstein played the piano.
He was a little man with small hands.
We were bombing Germany by then.
I went to see him in a dark warehouse
where a piano had been placed for his practice—
or whatever he did before a recital.
He signed the book I had with me—
it was called *Warsaw Ghetto*.
I later heard about him—
his affairs with young women—
if only I had known—but I was
in love with you.
Artur is dead;
and you, my darling,
the imprint of your face, alert like a deer—
oh god, it is eaten away—
the earth has taken it back;
but I listen to Artur—
he springs out of the grave—
his genius wired to this tape—
a sad trick of the neural pathways resonating flesh
and my old body remembers the way you touched me.

The Wound

The shock comes slowly
as an afterthought.

First you hear the words
and they are like all other words,

ordinary, breathing out of lips,
moving toward you in a straight line.

Later they shatter
and rearrange themselves. They spell

something else hidden in the muscles
of the face, something the throat wanted to say.

Decoded, the message etches itself in acid
so every syllable becomes a sore.

The shock blooms into a carbuncle.
The body bends to accommodate it.

A special scarf has to be worn to conceal it.
It is now the size of a head.

The next time you look,
it has grown two eyes and a mouth.

It is difficult to know which to use.
Now you are seeing everything twice.

After a while it becomes an old friend.
It reminds you every day of how it came to be.

The News

What have you to say to that
contorted gunned-down pile of rags
in a road; possibly nameless
even to the one who throws it
on a cart and pushes it away.

The discarded *New York Times*
is wrapped around your garbage,
a now wet, on-the-scene still
from someone's news camera,
stained with scraps from your kitchen.

And whose illusion that woman running
with a child? Already struck,
the machine gun crossing the line
of her body yet she does not fall
although she is already dead—

her history written backward—
There is no time to weep
for her. This was once the snot of semen,
the dim blue globe of the egg
moving through the fallopian tube.
That single body casting itself into the future.

That Day

Since then we've gone around the sun fifty times.
The sun itself has rushed on.
All the cells of my skin that you loved to touch
have flaked away and been renewed.
I am an epidermal stranger.
Even enormous factories. So much.
Even the railway station—
ball-wracked. Eliminated.
Now the dead may be pelletized,
disgorged as wafers in space.
Some may be sent to the sun in casks,
as if to Osiris.
Where is that day in Chicago
when we stood on a cement platform,
and I held your hand against my face,
waiting for a train in the warm light?
That given moment-by-moment light,
which, in a matter of hours from then,
had already traveled out of the solar system.

Things I Say to Myself while Hanging Laundry

If an ant, crossing on the clothesline
from apple tree to apple tree,
would think and think,
it probably could not dream up Albert Einstein.
Or even his sloppy mustache;
or the wrinkled skin bags under his eyes
that puffed out years later,
after he dreamed up that maddening relativity.
Even laundry is three-dimensional.
The ants cross its great fibrous forests
from clothespin to clothespin
carrying the very heart of life in their sacs or mandibles,
the very heart of the universe in their formic acid molecules.
And how refreshing the linens are,
lying in the clean sheets at night,
when you seem to be the only one on the mountain,
and your body feels the smooth touch of the bed
like love against your skin;
and the heavy sac of yourself relaxes into its embrace.
When you turn out the light,
you are blind in the dark
as perhaps the ants are blind,
with the same abstract leap out of this limiting dimension.
So that the very curve of light,
as it is pulled in the dimple of space,
is relative to your own blind pathway across the abyss.
And there in the dark is Albert Einstein
with his clever formula that looks like little mandibles
digging tunnels into the earth

and bringing it up, grain by grain,
the crystals of sand exploding
into white-hot radiant turbulence,
smiling at you, his shy bushy smile,
along an imaginary line from here to there.

Nuns at Lunch on the Bus

First they unzip the dark suitcase.
The more sedate one pulls out the plastic bag.
The other one zips the reticule and stretches
to put it up on the rack. With a smile she looks around.
It is a small congratulation.
Then they sit together.
A paper napkin is spread on each ample lap.
There is a momentary pause, almost breathless,
and then their delicate flesh fingers hold the sandwiches.
As they bite, they brush away the crumbs.
Their jaws, sensuous and steady, masticate the ham and cheese.
They wear draped heavy head covers,
dark coats and sensible dark oxford shoes.
Under their habits: beige skin, the beige of their plump bodies,
matrons who have given themselves.
Under their dark belts, below the layers of man-made fibers;
under their modest belly buttons,
the unscarred skins of their stomachs;
their organs, finally satiated, begin spasms of kneading,
softening the mass with pepsins and acids,
shoving it down into the bowels.
Now they pour coffee into Styrofoam
and lift it to their lips.
Then, mother of us all!
some little chocolate cakes come peeping forth
and are tucked into their benevolent mouths
with a gentle sucking and swallowing.
And then they tidy up.
The thermos top is screwed on. The lint brushed.

Paper napkins touched to their faces, their fingers.
The plastic pouch is stowed away.
And they settle to their deeper contemplations:
the body of truth, the temporal body, the vessel of love.

The Woman in the TV

The dark TV screen reflects the lamp;
the lamp and the windows.
And through the windows,
sunlight on the house next door.

In the dim room
inside the dark TV screen,
I see that a woman lives in there.
Sometimes she lies in bed all day.

Sometimes she thinks about the dark mountains;
the sharp outcroppings
that bristle with stunted pines,
the bare rock patches like diseased skin,
the trees like unwanted facial hairs.

She knows that the mountains can be seen
even at night; black against black.

The woman in there is heavy
like the raw-faced rocks;
the rocks that are bare even of snow,
when snow lies like a sickness,
like peeling skin on the pits and scars
of the thin soil in the crevices.

Sometimes the woman in the dark TV
pulls me to her.
"Draw the blinds," she whispers,

"and turn on the set—
so I can get out—
so we can be together."

The Sperm and the Egg

The sperm hate the egg.
They are afraid of it.
An ogress.
They clot the hot
red anteroom,
clinging to the walls.
She is blue and pulsing.
They are small and inadequate
and lose their tails.
Their chlorine milk begins to spoil.
But on the journey
when the shudder swept them
into an excited knot and
expelled them all together,
early sight scattered ahead of them.
They traveled like a shower of comets.
It was as if they were the universe.

The egg puts out her slimy pseudopod
and takes the sperm into the jelly.
The sperm is hysterical.
Now the egg is busy changing shape.
The sperm does not want to
be pulled apart into strings.
"Don't unravel me," it cries.
The egg does not hear it.
Deep inside the sperm
a seething hatred for the egg.
"When I had my tail,

I was free," the sperm cries.
It remembers the ultimate
vast trajectory.
It remembers them all crying,
"To be or not to be!"

Victorian Lamp on My Desk

From the lead angels strapped by the groins
to opposite sides of the lead column, you can only deduce
their desire to rise; their outstretched arms,
only the toes of their right feet touching the base,
their left legs stepping out into space.
But it is in their mouths,
open to drink the clouds they cannot reach,
and how their upper teeth show in a latent animal
despair, that they are frozen in the hell of artifice.

Bird in the Gilberts' Tree

What is that bird saying?
He is not just saying, "Here I am
and my nephews may not approach."
The entourages of plumage
in the courtly oak
are all another species.
"And you, my consort, my basket,
my broody decibels,
my lover in the lesser scales;
this is our tree, our vista,
our bagworms.
In short, tra la,
my territory.
Ah, but the sky straight up
is also mine.
This is the clear advantage
of my wings.
Also the sun;
my morning orange to you, my dear…
and so on."
This is what he sings.

Split, Conjugate, Whatever

The plastic cup is empty.
All of the frozen chocolate has been eaten.
The forest of the tongue giving succor
to the desires of its strange animals.
Tiny pronged heads of skin-tissue flowers
quiver with textural pleasure.
In the homely cave of the mouth,
ancient indigenous populations
begin to have sex and multiply.

The System

As shade preserves for a moment,
the dead mole—her purple velour coat,
the quiet dignity of her tough snout,
beetles carry her away
in decent discrete packages. In a slight measure,
make it possible for us to breathe
and walk every day over that pile,
as she liquefies to carrion.
And flies, good creatures that they are,
deposit a swarm of maggots in her,
to work in thrifty progression;
the fire of her particles
splitting their pale fat skins
growing along the lattice
with bristly hairs,
thousands of lenses,
suction cups of intractable feet,
as they labor in the bondage of form.

How It Came to Be

Once
a bear who couldn't sleep through the winter
fished the full moon out of a lake
and hung it in her cave.
"There," she said, "in essence,
can there be another like me?"
Echo came back, "Incandescence."
"That's it, bulb," she cried,
"you turn me on!"
And she went right out and got lit.
Edison obtained wind of this
and stole the whole thing,
and that's why it isn't dark any more.

A Love Like Ours

Once upon an avenue a small crack
smiled at a linden tree.
"I love your dappled shadow," it thought;
but only to itself.
The small crack stretched with pleasure.
The pure meld of the sun boiled
at its fragmented edges.
"How I crumble," the crack whispered,
"how the weight and the shock go through me.
I am a true MacAdam."
The linden tree shook itself in the jet stream.
It hummed with wings.
Male and female, pollen and pistil; it hummed.
Toward the equinox the air was filled with
a riding of seeds. They went in pushing crowds,
kicking and falling. They prickled the street
with their adolescent bursting.
In the morning the street cleaner,
gushing water, rolled over them
with thousands of bristles.
It brushed them along in a stream to the gutter.
One shy young linden seed was swept into the crack.
The crack gave a sigh.
At last it knew that the linden tree had noticed.
"A love like ours," said the crack,
"could split the street, could break up traffic!
Given time, it could even damage the sewer!"

Living Space

Up here, the folks who live in trailers
are often large fat folks but sometimes
they are wizened older men living alone.
The trailer is often close to the road
and often when the snow melts, a confusion
of cast-off tires, a sagging woodshed
and the brilliance of plastic that floated
from passing hot rods during the long
winter afflicts a naked sadness. Inside
the trailer, it will be over-warm with
wall-to-wall red carpeting. The kitchen
end, snug, with a maple table and chairs,
Electro-Perk and a tree of coffee mugs.

With certain trailers, toward evening
several men will be standing near the road.
A car has stopped and the ones in the car
lean out and those on the bare ground
in front of the trailer (the spot that will
later bloom with orange daylilies) will
seem to be settling some intricate problem
in motors. There will be another car and
a truck. The hood of a blowzy Plymouth
will be up. Regular traffic slows down to get
past and the people driving by, if they look,
can see hairy arms and thick fingers upending
cans of beer. The skinny owner of one of the
cars will be leaning back against the trailer
dragging on a cigarette and shouting "Hey, Bucky"

to a Buick that screeches to a stop and then guns on.
Or a trailer can be fronted with a small porch
with iron railings and pots of geraniums and
fluffy white curtains at the windows.
Its owners are almost never visible though
often it, too, is close to the road.
The trailers with children running in
and out usually have a beaten defeated
patch of grass and almost always a dog
tied up without any water or food in its
plastic dog bowls. For those on a low
fixed income, trailers are almost as
affordable as small houses used to be.

If they catch fire they are apt to burn
at white heat. Like other people, the
people who live in trailers may have
rectangular minds, modules for large
color TV's. The bottom-heavy young wives
may shop in the evening at Ames, their
small children playing hide-and-seek in
the racks of nylon pantsuits. They live
in another space. They have settled close
to the earth. They have retained their
rugged American rights to their own home.

Often elderly couples have traded a trailer
for a camper and drive south in cold weather,
their whimsical vehicles wagging down the
crowded lanes, while up front, their stiff
silver-haired profiles are pointed like
migrating lemmings toward that which is
always out there in the great American dark.

Good Friday on the Bus

Conversations behind you;
each wanting to get a lifetime
squeezed between Cleveland and Erie.
They drag it out,
the ordinary day to day;
sitting beside one another
without listening:
their families, their operations,
the virtues of the Pentecostal.
But the child
sitting next to you is silent.
After many miles
he is inspired to tell you
he has made an egg for his sister
but he has varnished it so
she can't crack it open.
He smiles.
Fields of stubble;
hay in vague shapes like kneeling animals.
Marbleized as a lake of ice, clouds,
separating pieces of puzzle drifting away.
Looking up into reflecting blue,
the camouflage of stars,
you think, as you must,
that what you see is the way it is,
the way it will always be.

For My Dead Red-haired Mother

I loved a red-haired girl.
Freud knew it was a wicked thing to do.
This is how all poems begin.
Sometime after the age of two
I beat the Adam in me black and blue.
Infant, wicked infant!
I threw my love outside
and grew into a bride.

You and I reflecting in our bones
the sea and sky,
we dressed ourselves as flesh,
we learned to lie.

Dearly beloved,
forgive me for that mean and meager self,
that now would mingle
but must first die.

Simplicity

I must retrace my exact steps on the crust,
or I will sink knee-deep in snow.
Kneeling to dip water from the open center of the brook—
between the ridged armies of black trees,
a splinter of light along the line of frost.
Clear as a printed map,
wrinkled skin on a cup of boiled milk—
the mountains of the moon, a full disk edging up.
Dreading all day to come here for this necessary water,
temperature dropping toward zero;
under the ice the water's muscular flow,
its insane syllables, is like a human voice.
Inside the house, sleep, sleep.
I brace myself to lift the weight on either hand.
Picking up my full kettle and bucket
and fitting my feet inside their frozen tracks,
I return under the risen moon,
following my shadow.

Columbus, Ohio

Practicing some silent underwater drift,
molded in plastic primary blue and yellow
bus station seats; like paper cutouts,
scissored replicas snipped from folded newspapers
to entertain a child,
these homeless bodies of men.
Hunched in layers, ten of them
asleep in hard cup chairs;
their feet in rotting shoes,
the time, three A.M.,
when suddenly one of them
stands up and stretches
and walks away yawning;
as if this is a decent home in the suburbs,
with children, arms and legs spread out
like baby starfish in their acrylic blankets.
As if he is leaving the soft mound of his wife's
secret body,
and going into their kitchen
to fill his thermos with hot coffee.
As if nothing is impossible,
as if it is an ordinary day.

That Moment

The mineral vapor rising from the sidewalks
on the shaded side where we met in the morning,
let loose from our acceptable ways
into a forbidden rendezvous.
Midwest, mid-'30s, U.S.A.,
the coffee shop beside a garage in Urbana, Illinois.
In the warm sleepwalking odor of a nearby bakery,
delicate mold from damp bricks, the deep murmur
of the prairie coming into us
like mica, like radiation, silently
tearing apart our fibers, altering our ganglia.
Under the marquee of the gas station,
a slapdash coffee stopover,
two tables in a lean-to beside the garage,
five cents a cup with buttered toast.
I remember every pore of your scarred face,
every gesture of your long fingers.
Those gifts so unexplored, passionate
thud of the portable Underwood,
fast as the fastest typist in the world;
those surreal novels now lying in a drawer,
lost to everyone but me.
I live in the mounting paper of loss.
Speaking to you, as we sat there
in the terror of our own violence,
even the odor of gasoline, provocative, sexual;
the glaze of this skew in time, twisting us
as at that moment the twisted iris
on the long translucent stalks were trembling

open, the folded tissues of themselves,
their opalescent throats, opening
to the unfolding of the miracle.

Finding Myself

Thursday, the 20th of July,
came to me and said,
I will give you this one elastic day.
Snap it shut or stretch it like bread dough.
So I put my hands in kneading and pulling.
It was a gauze-bag day.
The bluebell flower opened at the tip of its stalk.
I am body not equipped to take every flag downhill,
but looking at all the exits and entrances,
I chose white wine in a plain glass goblet,
and wearing a flannel nightgown,
I went barefoot into the uncut grass.
The temperature rose.
The yeast began to work.
Every spider took to the air.
The cells of my skin puffed and tugged
and with a great shout let go their tethers
until looking up I saw myself like a cloud,
like ectoplasm, like an angel
among the branches of trees.
Then peeling layer after layer
I went to it letting go,
until only the elemental worm remained
letting itself down
on a string of spittle.

Coffee and Sweet Rolls

When I remember the dingy hotels
where we lay reading Baudelaire,
your long elegant fingers, the nervous ritual
of your cigarette; you, a young poet working
in the steel mills; me, married
to a dull chemical engineer.
Fever of having nothing to lose;
no luggage, a few books, the streetcar.
In the manic shadow of Hitler, the guttural
monotony of war; often just enough money
for the night. Rising together in the clanking
elevators to those rooms where we lay like embryos;
helpless in the desire to be completed;
to be issued out into the terrible world.

All night, sighing and waking, insatiable.
At daylight, counting our change, you would go for coffee.
Then, lying alone, I heard the sirens,
the common death of everything and again
the little girl I didn't know
all in white in a white casket;
the boy I once knew, smashed with his motorcycle
into the pavement, and what was said,
"made a wax figure for his funeral,"
came into me. I had never touched the dead.
Always the lock unclicked and you were back,
our breakfast in a paper sack.
What I waited for was the tremor in your voice.
In those rooms with my eyes half open,

I memorized for that austere and silent woman
who waited in the future,
who for years survived on this fiction;
so even now I can see you standing thin and naked,
the shy flush of your rising cock pointed toward heaven,
as you pull down the dark window shade.

Scheherazade Is Mailed and Nailed in Five Days

At ten to seven on November 24, 1990,
Scheherazade is translated into the new world,
a little out of sync,
and still telling the story of Sinbad.
However, she arrives from Baghdad,
where an American soldier unrolled her
out of a cave in a hillside,
thinking she was a small dormant thing.
He was looking for shade, a little privacy,
in the act of writing a letter to his mother.
Scheherazade crept into the envelope
and here she is, reconstituted.
Well, they went for *I Dream of Jeannie,* so
who knows?
Yes, now she is afloat on the Alleghenies
in a second-floor flat with a genie mongrel,
still telling her stories
in order to save her head.
She looks into the animal's sad eyes.
It is just after a day of feasting.
The feast is done, the cheese rolls lie warmed over.
Alas, her caliph has been gone for hundreds of years.
Scheherazade has forgotten the executioner.
But she is still walking barefoot over the spikes of words.
How many veils drawn aside
to look into the pit of the caliph's heart?
His high-bridged nose, nostrils disdainful.
She thinks, will he never fall asleep?
But Scheherazade is, after all,

in love with her own voice.
She looks around this miraculous dwelling—
the cheap chest of drawers,
her now useless intimate apparel,
and the finally impotent rug.
She hears the dead caliph sigh.
Scheherazade has no choice.
In this place, my lord, she begins to fabricate,
sin is not so bad; in fact, it's the best
to be had. But it is overcast,
and my listeners are understandably bored.
She is referring to the dog.
What can I tell you about this old lamp,
you whose eyes have sucked into their skull?
She both knows and does not know that the caliph
is dead, that she is a figment herself in a story,
that the story is dying too and the storyteller.
Still, let me unclasp this brooch and touch the instrument.
It is the dance of a mouse, running across the sand,
or the memory of yourself
descending and ascending the marble stair,
leaning from the arched windows
to be other than you are,
to be elsewhere.
She is sitting on the rug.
The rug is kaput.
She's stuck.

November 25: Scheherazade is cheating at solitaire.
Now her stories are hewn out of newscasts.
The caliph is always looking the other way.
The dog sleeps, hooding his eyes of fire,
his demon's disguise.

Where is that sorcerer in torn clothes,
his cracked voice whining under the windows:
new lamps for old?
Instead, it snows.
Then the clouds are snatched away by whips
coming between the mountains.
Then the blue blind eye of nothing squints down.
She yawns, and lays out the cards.
Scheherazade and the dog are unaccountably fat.
The flying rug still does not raise them above the floor.
They sleep and wake only to eat or stand at the window,
to be amused by the chain of lights on the hills,
the moving cars, the infinite black veil.
Overhead the caliph's descendants fly
from continent to continent
with the smoothness of oil.
Now they control the world.
The former stories of Scheherazade
are small baggage for an old camel.

November 26: she continues chatting to the air,
inventing out of the new atmosphere:
to be the other on the Aleutian tundra,
to be a strong man dying on a golf course,
to be a drummer whose heart stops on the stage,
to be a middle-aged woman smoking her way through cancer,
to be a lover, loving in murderous rage.
And here she digresses.
The tundra, if it is bare, is a ghost place
where the sky falls into itself,
where the Arctic birds run into the wind to rise,
their feathers like fractals,
their nests hidden in the wildflowers.

And Scheherazade dances on bare feet.
She closes her eyes.
She forgets her other lives
like the one where the painted mime
wearing a G-string and pasties,
a coarse blond wig over his Egyptian hair,
drives at midnight to pick her up
at the door of the theater.
She murmurs, my caliph, as always, I hear
in the canyons and caves
the sighing of the poor.
And here in this place, the sirens,
the flashing lights
and the magic box,
the picture, always brilliant with blood
and always the echo of laughter.
To escape for a moment, she sings of the lover.
He is a dancer, he comes from the Mongol hordes
over the steppes, over the onyx ice.
His mother, a weaver of rugs,
rubs his skin with oil of roses.
He wears an embroidered vest,
silk leggings.
He leaps, he clicks his heels,
he clashes the scimitar.
His eyes are slant,
his cheeks cleaved to the bone;
his laugh is harsh. She listens—
Nothing.
He is gone a thousand moons
into the mountains of the forgotten.

He could be this man, living in a doorway,
or this man crossing the backyards
collecting bottles,
or this man, with a Saturday night special
in his hip pocket.
Forgive me, she sings, for loving this man in fear,
for my body that sleeps in an aggregate of deaths.
One story out of another,
so many inside one skin
like the spider's egg,
a world inside the self,
wrinkled, swelling, a heated balloon rising;
the voices, the costumes.
I am a multitude, sings the head.
Why have I only one body?

Time is falling inward,
an imploding sphere.
Scheherazade drones on. By now it is November 28th.
She snaps the switch
and lets the sorcerer's box speak for her.
These stories, my caliph, she hastens to say,
are repetitious,
the same old formula.
You will see, of course, misogyny, sadism,
violence, thieves in the streets, rape,
death of the spirit, blood, blood brothers.
It is all here.
She speaks of the merchandise,
bandits dancing with swords of fire, and then
war and the spoils of war. And afterward,
the trials, my caliph,
the usual trials, as yours,

always the hands cut off
and so forth. After a while,
again she is bored.
She grows deaf to the mechanical laughter.
Her multidimensional vision sees for miles,
multitudes frozen, the sorcerer's poison
pumping into their veins. They are all fat,
as the fattest Mogul. In front of their boxes
they fall asleep and snore.
But she tries to speak again.
A few grow very rich,
as you, my caliph; the rest become slaves.
Some lie down on the flat fitted rocks. Children
shiver in cast-out wrappings. It is all the same.
The women are tangled in the usual purdah,
as under you, my lord, the same ritual,
although there are small differences. Here each caliph's
caliph has a replacement, an inheritor, cunningly made
and hollow, where the magician hides.
Still she is bored. She begins to sigh
and she cannot dance. She feels no fugitive joy.
Once her stories were endless; now a gray wrack
of rags, she lies down, drunk; an habitual weeper.
The dead caliph cannot be charmed.
The flesh falls away under his splitting shroud.
The dog snores. At last Scheherazade comes face
to face with the executioner.
He comes through a thousand thousand doors.
They slam like the doors to the showers at Auschwitz.
You poets and lovers!
He faxes her a smile.
It was only a matter of time, he says.
You were always ours.

Once More

O my crows,
when you return in April,
your harsh voices,
your dark selves
rowing the raw air,
you males who made it home
to the mountain;
this shadow below you
in the orchard
is me,
triumphant,
listening
to rocks smash downstream
in the snowmelt.

Ordinary Words

1999

Good Advice

Here is not exactly here
because it passed by there
two seconds ago;
where it will not come back.
Although you adjust to this—
it's nothing, you say,
just the way it is.
How poor we are,
with all this running
through our fingers.
"Here," says the Devil,
"Eat. It's Paradise."

Up There

Belshazzar saw this blue
as he came into the walled garden,
though outside all was yellow,
sunlight striking the fractals of sand,
the wind striating the sand in riffles.

Land changes slowly, the fathoms
overhead accruing particles,
reflecting blue or less blue.

Vapor, a transient thing; a dervish
seen rising in a whirl of wind,
or brief cloud casting its changing shadow;
though below, the open-mouthed might stand
transfixed by mirage, a visionary oasis.

Nevertheless, this deep upside-down
wash, watercolor, above planted gardens,
tended pomegranates, rouged soles of the feet
of lovers lounging in an open tent;
the hot blue above; the harem
tethered and restless as camels.

This quick vision between walls, event,
freak ball, shook jar of vapor,
all those whose eyes were not gouged out,
have looked up and seen within the cowl
this tenuous wavelength.

Words

Wallace Stevens says,
"A poet looks at the world
as a man looks at a woman."

I can never know what a man sees
when he looks at a woman.

That is a sealed universe.

On the outside of the bubble
everything is stretched to infinity.

Along the blacktop, trees are bearded as old men,
like rows of nodding gray-bearded mandarins.
Their secondhand beards were spun by female gypsy moths.

All mandarins are trapped in their images.

A poet looks at the world
as a woman looks at a man.

1941

I wore a large brim hat
like the women in the ads.
How thin I was: such skin.
Yes. It was Indianapolis;
a taste of sin.

You had a natural Afro;
no money for a haircut.
We were in the seedy part;
the buildings all run-down;
the record shop, the jazz
impeccable. We moved like
the blind, relying on our touch.
At the corner coffee shop,
after an hour's play, with our
serious game on paper,
the waitress asked us
to move on. It wasn't much.

O mortal love, your bones
were beautiful. I traced them
with my fingers. Now the light
grows less. You were so angular.
The air darkens with steel
and smoke. The cracked world
about to disintegrate,
in the arms of my total happiness.

How They Got Her to Quiet Down

When the ceiling plaster fell in Aunt Mabel's kitchen
out in the country (she carried her water uphill
by bucket, got all her own wood in),
that was seventy-five years ago, before she
took her ax and chopped up the furniture.
Before they sent her to the asylum.
Shafe, father of the boys (she didn't have a girl),
was running around with a loose woman.
Earlier Shafe threw the baby up against the ceiling.
"Just tossing him," he said. Little Ustie came down
with brain fever. In two days that child was dead.
Before that, however, the boys all jumped
on the bed upstairs and roughhoused so
that one night the ceiling fell in;
all lumped on the floor. The kitchen was a sight.
But those kids did not go to the poorhouse.
Grandma was elected to take them.
Mabel's sisters all said, "Ma, you take the boys."
Beauty is as beauty does. Grandma chased them
with a switch until they wore a bare path
around her last cottage. Grandma was small
and toothless, twisted her hair in a tight bun.
After she smashed the furniture, Mabel tried
to burn the house down. Years later when they
let Mabel out of the asylum, she was so light
you could lift her with one hand.
Buddy took her in and she lay on the iron bed
under a pieced quilt. "Quiet as a little bird," he said.

So What

For me the great truths are laced with hysteria.
How many Einsteins can we tolerate?
I leap into the uncertainty principle.
After so many smears you want to wash it off with a laugh.
Ha ha, you say. So what if it's a meltdown?
Last lines to poems I will write immediately.

Male Gorillas

At the doughnut shop
twenty-three silver backs
are lined up at the bar,
sitting on the stools.
It's morning coffee and trash day.
The waitress has a heavy feeling face,
considerate with carmine lipstick.
She doesn't brown my fries.
I have to stand at the counter
and insist on my order.
I take my cup of coffee to a small
inoffensive table along the wall.
At the counter the male chorus line
is lined up tight.
I look at their almost identical butts,
their buddy hunched shoulders,
the curve of their ancient spines.
They are methodically browsing
in their own territory.
This data goes into that vast
confused library, the female mind.

So What's Wrong?

Here it is, a green world
and all of these millions
living in the dust.
It's like a dog with a chain
that's just as long as this worn
path around the post.
How the dog loves the hand
that brings it water;
the voice up there,
almost out of reach, that says,
"Here is your food.
Nice dog."
While it eats, like a dream,
the voice goes away;
and there is the path
around the post.
Joyful dog, something,
somewhere, is so wonderful.
And at night, the dog
lies down and its muscles
remember the ferns,
the hot smell of the field
sloping downhill,
the clouds breaking,
and that light,
like mist, like smoke;
the strange reflected light
of a dead moon.

Yes, Think

Mother, said a small tomato caterpillar to a wasp,
why are you kissing me so hard on my back?
You'll see, said the industrious wasp, deftly inserting
a package of her eggs under the small caterpillar's skin.
Every day the small caterpillar ate and ate the delicious
tomato leaves. I am surely getting larger, it said to itself.
This was a sad miscalculation. The ravenous hatched
wasp worms were getting larger. O world, the small
caterpillar said, you were so beautiful. I am only a small
tomato caterpillar, made to eat the good tomato leaves.
Now I am so tired. And I am getting even smaller. Nature
smiled. Never mind, dear, she said. You are a lovely link
in the great chain of being. Think how lucky it is to be born.

Then

That summer, from the back porch,
we would hear the storm like a train,
the Doppler effect compressing the air;
the rain, a heavy machine, coming up
from below the orchard, rushing toward us.
My trouble was I could not keep you dead.
You entered even the inanimate,
returning in endless guises.
And that winter an ermine moved into the house.
It was so cold the beams cracked.
The ermine's fur was creamy white
with the last half of the tail soot black.
Its body about ten inches long,
it slipped through small holes.
It watched us from a high shelf in the kitchen.
In our loss we accepted the strange shape of things
as though it had a meaning for us,
as though we moved slowly over the acreage,
as though the ground modulated like water.
The floors and the cupboards slanted to the West,
the house sinking toward the evening side of the sky.
The children and I sitting together waiting,
there on the back porch, the massive engine
of the storm swelling up through the undergrowth,
pounding toward us.

One Thought

Accompanied
by many pictures,
the words
swelled and shrank.
The brain
flashed intermittently,
easily explained
in a simple collider.
The energy of nothing
smashed into the
energy of something.
There was complicity
in our smiles.
One thought—
I cannot live without you,
O brief and inconceivable other.

Sorting It Out

Falsely soft, infinitely far,
the chlorophyll machine.
Each socket knocked by a photon
from the mother star.

It's the trees and their green flesh.
Listen, our fingers feel the hiss.
The great blue whale
picks up the sonar.

This obsession with invisible things.

But the concrete with its gray crumbling smile
is like a factual male.
Drive your car into me, it suggests:
I'm no bloody vagina.

The concrete stretches for miles;
the turrets with guns in position.

So Be It

Look, this string of words
is coming out of my mouth,
or was. Now it's coming
out of this pen whose ink
came from Chattanooga.
Something tells me
Chattanooga was a chief.
He came out of his mother's
body. He pushed down
the long tube that got
tighter and tighter until
he split it open and stuck
his head out into a cold
hollow. Holding his belly
by a bloody string he
screamed, "I am me,"
and became a cursive
mark on a notepad that
was a former tree taken
with other trees in the
midst of life and mutilated
beyond all remembrance
of the struggle from seed
to cambium; the slow
dying roots feeling for some
meaning in the eroded
soil; the stench of decay
sucked into the chitin
of scavengers, becoming

alien to xylem and phloem,
the vast vertical system
of reaching up. For there
is nothing that is nothing,
but always becoming
something; flinging itself;
leaping from level to level.

In the Next Galaxy

Spring Beauties

The abandoned campus,
empty brick buildings and early June
when you came to visit me;
crossing the states midway,
the straggled belts of little roads;
hitchhiking with your portable typewriter.
The campus, an academy of trees,
under which some hand, the wind's I guess,
had scattered the pale light
of thousands of spring beauties,
petals stained with pink veins;
secret, blooming for themselves.
We sat among them.
Your long fingers, thin body,
and long bones of improbable genius;
some scattered gene as Kafka must have had.
Your deep voice, this passing dust of miracles.
That simple that was myself, half conscious,
as though each moment was a page
where words appeared; the bent hammer of the type
struck against the moving ribbon.
The light air, the restless leaves;
the ripple of time warped by our longing.
There, as if we were painted
by some unknown impressionist.

Seed

Corn is universal,
so like a Roman senator.
Its truths are silk tassels.
True its ears are sometimes
rotten, impure.
But it aspires in vast acres,
rectangular spaces,
to conspire with every pollinator
and to bear for the future
in its yellow hair.

And what are your aspirations,
oh my dears,
who will wear into tatters
like the dry sheaves
left standing, shuttering
in November's wind;
my Indian corn, my maize,
my seeds for a ruined world;
Oh my daughters.

In the Next Galaxy

Things will be different.
No one will lose their sight,
their hearing, their gallbladder.
It will be all Catskills with brand-
new wraparound verandas.
The idea of Hitler will not
have vibrated yet.
While back here,
they are still cleaning out
pockets of wrinkled
Nazis hiding in Argentina.
But in the next galaxy,
certain planets will have true
blue skies and drinking water.

Rising

In the government offices the rules and regulations
regarding erosion of beaches moves from one file to another.
The sand whispers back into the undertow.
At the South Pole, part of the frozen continent splits
and melts, eating into the ice pack.
Along the Eastern Seaboard a house on the ocean
is lifted on stilts. It walks into the water.
The piles driven deep into the sand are at last exposed,
their thin bones fragile as tiny starfish.
The windows, blank eyes of dead seagulls,
catch the phosphorescence in the choppy waves.
The waves are as even as furrows in a cornfield.
But the house is moving in the opposite direction.
How mild the evening is. No one would suppose
that the house is going out with the tide.

Genesis

Cylinder sacks of water filling the oceans,
endless bullets of water,
skins full of water rolling and tumbling
as we came together.
As though light broke us apart.
As though light came with the rubble of words,
though we die among the husks of remembering.
It is as we knew it would be
in the echoes of endless terminals,
in the slow scaled guises of ourselves
when we came together in the envelopes of ourselves,
the bare shadow, the breath of words invisible;
as slight errors repeating themselves;
as degradation passes like madness through a crowd.
It was not ordained.
It was one drop of salt water against another.

As It Is

In this squat body,
the most delicate things;
host of ravishing flagella.
Out of the Far East,
dormant diseases
waiting their turn.
The cavity under the skull
not proliferating
but shoring up, shrinking.
Outside, the air, lightly
polluted as everywhere;
the crime rate steady
and rising. Oh, world,
I said, feeling with my feet
her soft pubic hair,
the uncut grass outside
my kitchen door,
her benign pulse hot
on my skin, the apple trees'
spent petals letting go
in the slight wind, gyrating
down like snow. Oh world, I said.

Bits of Information

While her minuscule fledglings, each slightly
larger and heavier than a bumblebee,
are rising out of the woven handbag of their nest,
this hummingbird is sipping jewelweed.
It's all that's left. She should be at magenta
and scarlet, not this small orange and yellow
flowering lip. The jewelweed shoots its seeds
with buckshot energy. Its chemistry once used
to soothe the blisters etched by poison ivy.
The female hummingbird is heavier than he
and darker without the ruby at the throat.
Still hovering in air, her wing beats blur invisible.
While he, a smaller body, father of the fledglings,
has gone free; an irresponsible bachelor
since that quick act of sex; her single parenting
is adequate. The fledglings emulate and follow her.
This winged woman Icarus never dreamed of,
will cross the Gulf of Mexico, living on stored up fat.

Before the Blight

The elms stretched themselves in indolent joy,
arching over the street that lay in green shadow
under their loose tent.
And the roses in Mrs. Mix's yard pretzeled up her trellis
with pink Limoges cabbage blooms like Rubens' nudes.
My lips whispered over the names of things
in the meadows, in the orchard, in the woods,
where I sometimes stood for long moments
listening to some bird telling me of the strangeness of myself;
rocked in the sinewy arms of summer.

Poems

When you come back to me
it will be crow time
and flycatcher time,
with rising spirals of gnats
between the apple trees.
Every weed will be quadrupled,
coarse, welcoming
and spine-tipped.
The crows, their black flapping
bodies, their long calling
toward the mountain;
relatives, like mine,
ambivalent, eye-hooded;
hooting and tearing.
And you will take me in
to your fractal meaningless
babble; the quick of my mouth,
the madness of my tongue.

Breathing

By day the brook is subsumed
under a rush of summer;
voices of motors and warblers,
rubbing steel of the swings;
the shouting across the road
for dogs, for children.
Even when you go down to its bed,
it gives way to this busy noise.

A gang of crows and everything's
overhead; chipping sparrows,
spin of their stubborn trills;
slip of the maples tangled
together; great mops scrubbing
the air; the slosh of wind.

But at night, the water lipping
below the voice of your breathing,
or the catch of your breath,
its stopped stillness; when
you wake with a start and listen
for the sound of the spill
beginning again, braiding itself,
and the fall of rock on rock
sucked down in its liquid mouth.

On the Slow Train Passing Through

Here's Moody Furniture and the town of Moody. Also the display
for Temple Chemicals, a wire fence, some rubble and bare ground.
Privy to this endless street along the tracks, I watch
ongoing traffic move around something on the road.
It's a man on the center line lying on his back;
a woman bending down to touch him.
The cars move on. The train slides past.
And yet, in Roanoke, Virginia, in 1907, when grandma's
house was on fire, the passing trolley stopped and everyone
got off and ran up the hill to help, even though there was no easy water.
Three members of a Baptist choir endangered their whiskers,
their business attires, their waistcoats and themselves, to carry
out grandma's organ and her cherry sitting room furniture.
Although the upstairs burned through the roof and my mother's
new treadle sewing machine and her new tailored suit were
among the traumatic losses; they all did what they could.
It was the dignity of a communal disaster. No one was going
anywhere more important than that. The trolley horse had been
unhitched and loosely tethered to graze and eventually they heard
the far off sound of the approaching fire brigade. Meanwhile,
grandpa had been fetched from the foundry. Afterward, those women
who had done all they could to save my grandma's belongings,
total strangers, each in her own way commiserated with grandma.
The men washed at the pump and they all walked down the hill.
The conductor hitched up the trolley and they went on with their
     regular day.

Eden, Then and Now

In '29 before the dust storms
sandblasted Indianapolis,
we believed in the milk company.
Milk came in glass bottles.
We spread dye-colored butter,
now connected to cancer.
We worked seven to seven
with no overtime pay;
pledged allegiance every day,
pitied the starving Armenians.
One morning in the midst of plenty,
there were folks out of context,
who were living on nothing.
Some slept in shacks
on the banks of the river.
This phenomenon investors said
would pass away.
My father worked for the daily paper.
He was a union printer;
lead slugs and blue smoke.
He worked with hot lead
at a two-ton machine,
in a low-slung seat;
a green-billed cap
pulled low on his forehead.
He gave my mother a dollar a day.
You could say we were rich.
This was the Jazz Age.
All over the country

the dispossessed wandered
with their hungry children,
harassed by the law.
When the market broke, bad losers
jumped out of windows.
It was time to lay an elegant table,
as it is now; corporate paradise;
the apple before the rot caved in.
It was the same worm
eating the same fruit.
In fact, the same Eden.

Wanting

Wanting and dissatisfaction
are the main ingredients
of happiness.
To want is to believe
there is something worth getting.
Whereas getting only shows
how worthless the thing is.
And this is why destruction
is so useful.
It gets rid of what was wanted
and so makes room
for more to be wanted.
How valueless is the orderly.
It cries out for disorder.
And life that thinks it fears death,
spends all of its time
courting death.
To violate beauty
is the essence of sexual desire.
To procreate is the essence of decay.

At the Ready

Under the aerial squadron,
wheat fields are ready
for McCormick reapers.
The planes pass over
copulating mice;
grasshoppers, programmed like
investors on the margin;
ants, relocating tons of soil;
and snakes with useful toads
still kicking in their guts.
These items are not among
the criteria for observation.

From overhead, the planes,
geometrically spaced,
cast long stippled shadows
on the rippling fields;
dark flashes like a military code,
like an urgent monotonous message
beamed to the combat zone,
repeating instructions to the already dead.

A Pair

The black and white cat
means to get off
the screened-in porch.
Castrated but suave,
he lives with this older woman
whose husband, dead thirty years,
secretly puts his cheek to hers
in a dime store photograph.
The children no longer visit.
The cat holds all the threads
of her detonated psyche.
He is the master key without
a lock. She picks him up.
The porch screen has been mended.
He thinks there are the old openings.
Birds, insects leap
out of the flecked light.
Inside the screen, her hands
stroke his electric body.

What We Don't Know

It is Wednesday. My day off.
The neighborhood quiet.
My cats pulse, tails up,
like submarines scanning the surface.
Last night through the lifted window,
melting snow released an ozone sting.
Last night I twisted in the arms
of a heavy book on radioactive pollution.
I have gone through its troubled corridors.
In its inner labyrinths, I have eaten
the survivors, the mutilated bodies,
the cancers of children; like fruitcake
sliced in the kitchen at 3 A.M.;
all this only whets the appetite;
the insomniac leaning
against the doorjamb.
Now it's 11 A.M. on Wednesday;
the area, ordinary, as usual.
Fog beads along the wires.
Last night's implant in the brain,
useless information after the facts,
like the gradual glitch of shifting faults,
almost unnoticed; in the way
two birds streak through the air,
in the wing language of April,
above them the dark metaphor
of two soundless fighter jets.

At Eighty-three She Lives Alone

Enclosure, steam-heated; a trial casket.
You are here; your name on a postal box;
entrance into another place like vapor.
No one knows you. No one speaks to you.
All of their cocks stare down their pant legs
at the ground. Their cunts are blind. They
barely let you through the check-out line.
Have a nice day. Plastic or paper?

Are you origami? A paper folded swan,
like the ones you made when you were ten?
When you saw the constellations, lying
on your back in the wet grass,
the soapy pear blossoms drifting
and wasting, and those stars, the burned out ones
whose light was still coming in waves;
your body was too slight.
How could it hold such mass?
Still on your lips the taste of something.

All night you waited for morning, all morning
for afternoon, all afternoon for night;
and still the longing sings.
Oh, paper bird with folded wings.

Getting to Know You

We slept into one another.
The mattress sloped us to your side.
We shared three daughters.
Miraculous dull day to day
breakfast and dinner.

But compared to all the optic scanning,
the nerve ends of retrospection
in my thirty years of knowing you
cell by cell in my widow's shawl,
we have lived together longer
in the discontinuous films of my sleep
than we did in our warm parasitical bodies.

Thus, by comparison, when the palms
of our hands lay together exchanging oils
and minuscule animals of the skin;
we were relative strangers.

Air

Through the open window, a confusion
of gasoline fumes, lilacs, the green esters of grass.
Edward Waite rides the lawn mower.
Each summer his voice is more stifled. His emphysema is worse.
"Three packs a day," he says, still proud of the fact.
Before he got sick, he drove semis across the country.
Every two weeks he drives his small truck up the mountain.
He mows in long rows fitting swath to cut swath, overlapping the width.
To please me he saves the wild paintbrush along the edge.
Stripped to the waist, I see he has hung his blue shirt
on my clothesline to dry out the sweat.
The shirt, with its arms upraised, filled with the body of air,
is deeply inhaling, exhaling its doppelgänger breath.

Sorrow and No Sorrow

We eat through tubes of time
as the cockroach,
as the apple and the codling moth,
as worms of neutrinos;
and what is not there
is always more than there.
As the dropped fawn,
dappled and cinnamon;
as the wind lays the fern aside
and carries the fawn's milk breath
over the ravenous field
on its indifferent tongue.

Points of Vision

In February the hills of Niguel flush green,
a rush of new grass fine as baby hair.
Shizu drives out with her easel.
The red-tailed hawks are working
the folds and wrinkles where
the ground squirrels hide.
Tormented by crows, three hawks
spiral up and drift under and over,
becoming small as sparrows.
Above them a jet streaks in the cumulus.
Frenetic ground squirrels
pop in and out of their burrows.
Now they're motionless.
Now the enlarged shadow
of a descending hawk
sweeps over the hummocks,
like a blind hand feeling its way.
Shizu prepares her watercolors.

Train Ride

All things come to an end;
small calves in Arkansas,
the bend of the muddy river.
Do all things come to an end?
No, they go on forever.
They go on forever, the swamp,
the vine-choked cypress, the oaks
rattling last year's leaves,
the thump of the rails, the kite,
the still white stilted heron.
All things come to an end.
The red clay bank, the spread hawk,
the bodies riding this train,
the stalled truck, pale sunlight, the talk;
the talk goes on forever,
the wide dry field of geese,
a man stopped near his porch
to watch. Release, release;
between cold death and a fever,
send what you will, I will listen.
All things come to an end.
No, they go on forever.

Sorrow

Living alone the feet turn voluptuous,
cold as sea water, the thin brine
of the blood reaches them slowly;
their nubby heads rub one another.
How can you love them and yet
how live without them?
Their shoes lined up like caskets
in which they lie all day
dead from one another.
In the night
each foot has nothing to love
but the other foot.

Lines

Voice, perhaps you are the universe,
the hum of spiders.
If on the mountain a single bear
comes into the orchard;
much less, the husk of a locust
drops from the currant bush;
or the wind rattles a loose clapboard,
exchanging one skin for another—
it is the self longing to cross the barrier.
Sensing the visitors who hide among us,
the air enters and takes away.
Sharp as the odor of fresh sawdust,
the color of lost rooms,
those erotic odors, angst of brevity;
like crossing your thighs
in a spasm of loneliness.

Tongues

To mortify the spirit I once attended
some classes of beginning French, et cetera.
And have I climbed toward heaven or descended?
It does not matter. I am not one
whom God can hope to save by dying twice.
I am lost among the words of sacrament.
What can I say but that I love the wind,
and I am shaken when it shakes and scatters
the stuttering leaves on the insensible pavement.

To Try Again

"Tremble," says the sword-grass, leaning over the water.
"Oh yes," the water-fractals sing, writhing in temporal ecstasy,
"Toward is inevitable. Fall to the center."
"Rushing, always rushing," sighs the larch, brushing the sky.
"Your roots are not deep enough. Try harder.
Apply yourself." On the milkweed, the larvae of the monarchs
grow against the pulsing heliosphere. "We must die
and be born again. The clouds of our endless selves
image the chrysalis. Yes, to become is the meaning."
"Look," says the void. "What meaning? Be thou me."

Mantra

When I am sad
I sing, remembering
the redwing blackbird's clack.
Then I want no thing
except to turn time back
to what I had
before love made me sad.

When I forget to weep,
I hear the peeping tree toads
creeping up the bark.
Love lies asleep
and dreams that everything
is in its golden net;
and I am caught there, too,
when I forget.

In the Dark

Accepting

Half-blind, it is always twilight.
The dusk of my time and the nights
are so long, and the days of my tribe
flash by, their many colored cars
choking the air, and I lie like a shah
on my divan in this 21st-century
mosque, indifferent to my folded
flesh that falls in on itself,
almost inert, remembering crossing
the fields, turning corners, coming
home to the lighted windows,
the pedestrian years of it, accepting
from each hand the gifts,
without knowing why they were
given or what to make of them.

Another Day

The fleeting high that lifts you
at six A.M. after a cup of coffee;
or is it that you've lived into another day?
After the sun sets and you look out there
on the dark that is neither down nor up,
not even the patterns of stars can tell you where.

Still, light comes and lies on your skin
like the membrane of a delicate egg.
You do not need to feel anything,
enclosed in this sac: etched lineage,
ball of twine, fractal of lost feathers.

Full Moon

My problem is not enough
or too much sleep;
uneasy sleep, apnea sleep.
Is it the hole in the ozone?
That snooze effect?
Another full moon,
our divided self,
out there baring
its hard flesh.
The spotlight
on the world's goiter;
the gland that affects
our tidal blood.
Every river vein
lifts like an eyebrow
with the pull.
A globe fish
pronged in weeds;
black stiff hairs
against the blind sky.
The hemlocks, the woods,
a rising slope;
matte wig of the mountain.
The evening birds
diving from branch to branch;
or full spread, a nightjar,
ready to throttle
to another nightjar.

Bennington Bus Stop

She gets off the bus and they kiss.
It's a hard embrace.
Then he walks on the balls of his feet
like a basketball star,
and contorts himself into the driver's
seat of a compact car.
She stands outside,
averts her face,
wipes her lips with the back of her hand
as if to erase a smear,
or a breath of dust on a photograph
album stacked in the future.
Then she slips into her place
beside him and everything is sure
as the weekend, as sure
as their nineteen-year-old bodies,
as sure as death
that sweetens their given grace.

Bianca

On the cement belt over the cement playground,
buses, cars, trucks, move from one side
to the other. Hyphens of traffic;
dashes from nowhere to nowhere.
We sit on the benches under the sycamore.

And in the almost indestructible play-yard,
Bianca finds a throng of dandelions.
Her tenderness gathers them up.
Her yellow hair hanging over them,
her astringent herbal essence.
Her small hands filling passion's bitter cup.

Walter, Upon Looking Around

"Men are getting extinct,"
says my grandson, Walter.
"Look how little I am;
and I'm the only boy in the family.
I hardly ever see a boy,"
he says, warming to his subject.

Clay

Tuesday and I am still in the coils
of this serpent masking as a vein.
It has swallowed so much. I am the half-
swallowed toad still kicking in the throat.

It's like I walk to the end of the world
and come to a wall. There is no top to the wall.
It goes up forever. My body adds itself to the bricks.

Cause and Effect

Once a stick who was tired
of being beaten against everything
lay down on the fagot pile.
"Let me ascend to heaven," it snarled.
Presently wood smoke rose
from the poet's chimney.

Border

Driving through Indiana;
creeks wriggle alongside the highway,
incidental,
like, "Oh yes,
someone used to wade there."
A knot of deformed trees,
almost too old-fashioned,
remnants of a farm, discontinued merchandise.
But it's mostly lost streams,
weed-trees, and a loneliness that hints
of automatic two-car-garage doors and zoysia grass;
small, well-kept lawns and sudden streets,
and identical houses around a factory
that sprawls the way small colleges used to spread themselves out:
lawns, flower beds, groundsmen with mowing machines.
The quiet authority of culture.

Almost the Same

When it's all over,
the ravishing lines,
the simple innuendos,
something implied beyond the self.
As if like the jewelweed
you have scattered yourself
God knows where,
and you are positioned to be a silhouette
against the snow.
And where is this poem going,
if not into stasis?
All words on stone or papyrus,
linen or pulp,
written in some loved alphabet,
thousands of years old.
Scribes, and the counting for taxes,
or the river's seasonal flooding.
Ships drifting,
and the same, or
almost the same
sun.

Currents

Something about a flock of birds toward evening.
The weather report sleet, snow.
The hot males riding ahead,
the swamp ridged in last year's cattails.
Ego, vanity, the male strut.
Oh, that burr and sweetest whistle,
their hearts pumped with thrush steroids.
In another week, perhaps a quick melt
and we'll hear them clinging to the old stalks,
staking out their claims
while from the south
the slow shadow of the migrating females
like Cleopatra's barge,
the oars dipping,
the fringed canopy
like clouds of sweet rain
rippling behind.
The eternal tribal ritual,
the dense flock, undulating
packet of the future—
great sperm bank of the galaxy,
the billions of the separate
that gathers itself into the one,
summer after summer.

Elsie's Brooks

It's hard to carry you around inside me
without the real sound of your voice
that was not always praising me,
and did I say enough to you
concerning those peripheral things
I knew you cared about?
The lazy time was lazy in my voice.
There were so many silences.
I think, do you hear me now
speaking for both of us?
Thinking along those paths
you walked more often alone,
going up in the woods behind your house
and farther up, where you found
blue hepatica, bone white trillium,
and the source of the springs
that had spread out down the slope
in a broad swamp. You worked the water free
of years of rot and silt and dug those brooks
back to their rock beds where now the clear
water runs downhill. Your muddy wet
tennis shoes were always lined up
on the porch where you would come
down to change out of one soaked
and mud-filled pair into a dry mud-caked
replica, and after a cup of tea, you'd go
back up there to drain the mountain.

Riding the Bubble

Poetry that uses non sequiturs
which are transformations
in the direction of Zen,
as the hyper-angle in Vasko
Popa's "Prudent Triangle"—
a linguistic arrangement
of infinity—
is intriguing to us

with our near sighted vision
frozen along the contiguous;
our popular choice,
a self-inflating universe.

And so far, at the farthest
visible edge, the bubble appears
to bend; light appears to speed up
because it curves away from
where it was.

The still somewhat
unexplained weak force
possibly becoming aggregate;
separating masses,
galaxies slipping
out of sight in opposite directions.

Today

October's brilliance is half gone from the avenues,
or lies on lawns and gutters;
and rain, the blessed curse
in dissolved frost, yields ropes of mirrors.
The cheap, chiming clock says almost ten.

Then why this happiness in muted things?
Some equation of time and space,
a slowed perception of the battered brain
strips back like leaves to unexpected glittering.

The Self and the Universe

This is not poetic language,
but it is the language of poetry.
At night, on the page,
the lines change
like the chaotic patterns of your eyes,
these holes into space.
You lie on your bed,
the snowball earth,
a frozen chance;
the little knowledge of dust lanes,
the ghastly voter frauds of the last election,
and the late spring snows,
pots of forced purple crocuses.
How fragile and enduring the words.
This is the self and the universe.
This is the wild sweep of the sun,
that mysterious molecule;
this clutter of rocks, dust,
and lighter elements, like your fingernails;
like the configurations of the spiral lines
on the soles of your feet,
undeciphered.

Heaven

Before we knew the true
polyhedral vision
and reduced all possibility
to a perfectly fulfillable eternity;
ignorance hung
like a bat of viscous glue;
upside down—
beautiful blind insectivore.

Ice

Are you persuaded that dormant flies, moles,
bears, and all the rest, as the wheel slows down,
are as we, in the interstices of love? There toll
the small bells of their sleeping souls. We
do not sleep. We die and are reborn and die again,
as the annual flowers, in the pulse of pain.

Love, for a bridge of sighs, from my winter to yours,
to hang with icicle garlands that the wind may crash
and clang among. Then in our death's time, showers
of cold roses and snow poppies and the tracery of blue-white
forget-me-nots carved of the purest ice may lash
us with the sting of memory.

How Can I?

Saying it over and over,
the eyes forget
the subtle alphabet,
or calligraphy,
the sweet nuances of style,
and fall to hieroglyphics.
And the body, asleep,
walks along the Nile
planting papyrus,
a basket to catch words;
the feet caked with dust,
the poor thighs heavy,
and the entire torso squat,
not anyone you would remember.
And yet,
far away, lying on a foam mat,
the blind self thinks
how can I live like this?

In the Free World

The teenager in for involvement
in murder and dismemberment
feels unjustly treated. He says,
"Why I never even got my driver's
license." He refers to his offense
as "catching his case." He feels
no remorse for burying the skinned
and beheaded female victim.

A short time ago it was only thirty,
but now for under a hundred dollars
you can get a license enabling you
to legally sell weapons; handguns,
machine guns, you are an automatic
licensed dealer in automatics.

And the Mexican government,
after betraying the native Mexican
farmers, sends helicopters in
to bomb them and quell dissatisfaction.
It's quicker and maybe more humane
than just starving them. After
the insurrection, the dead Indians
lying in their own blood were found
to be carrying carved wooden guns,
just pieces of carved wood.

Interim

Like the radiator that sits
in the kitchen passing gas;
like the mop with its head
on the floor, weeping;
or the poinsettia that pretends
its leaves are flowers;
the cheap paint peels
off the steamed walls.
When you have nothing to say,
the sadness of things
speaks for you.

Euphoria

This euphoria,
this sunlight in February,
these lines to myself.
Not even the ivy that looped
across my bedroom window;
and what were those summer mornings?
One grows up in a brick house
on a winding street
in Indianapolis.
Wildflowers on the slope
behind the house, the elms,
and beyond that, the railroad
with its blinking lights
and long Doppler whistle
of the evening train.
Hepatica, dog-toothed violet,
spring beauties.
And the elms, that formed green arches
over the street all the way
to the Baptist Church,
and three long blocks
from my grandmother's.
That blue sky, that delicate wind.

Clotheslines

Lines yes, clotheslines,
where the laundry lashes the bitter air.
The martyr, who thinks she is a female
born to scrub board.
But then there is the casting line
with the barbed hook flashing out of the shadow.
And then there are the water walkers,
and the gauze of dragonflies.
The blind grow inconsistent.
Words like midges swarming in a cloud
move between the clotheslines
where the flycatchers twitch their tails.
They gather them with a snap
of their darling beaks.
Or, like the whale's fabulous sieve of baleen,
feed on the microcosm of the world.

Margaret Street

In September Margaret Street
waits for the comet.
No one but the earth knows that it is coming.

And the earth with its extravagant garment
like Salome's veils
gyrates in the sensual clasp.

In September the deepest basins
gush up their silt.
On Margaret Street the neighbors take out their trash.

It is Sunday. Each delayed moment
is wrested out of the seething mass.

On Mitchell Ave, where vision was still brilliant,
I suffered small indignities.
Ignorance lies always in the past.

O language that follows like the comet's tail;
the rubble of senseless longing
for what was.

What Is a Poem?

Such slight changes in air pressure,
tongue and palate,
and the differences in teeth.
Transparent words.
Why do I want to say ochre,
or what is green-yellow?
The sisters of those leaves on the ground
still lisp on the branches.
Why do I want to imitate them?

Having come this far
with a handful of alphabet,
I am forced,
with these few blocks,
to invent the universe.

Menty Ears Ago

Menty ears ago the dummer was sappy in my harms
but I was yawning and spawning and twenty.
What tears I let down in my beers of plenty.
What sleet in his goat's beard tickled my sweat.
Not a fret left its own key, every morning
when we were ferning and fronding and yorning.

The Wailing Wall

On and off the air spits a little snow.
This changed water is so beautiful.
I think your bones are also beautiful.
Remote body, trembling with the rush
of traffic; body of altered elements.
You are my beggar's sack, the weight
of this slipping shadow, this eclipse.
You evaporate as these words evaporate.

Crows pump the air across this space;
even they are awkward in the cold.
Their grace disintegrates but not like yours.
Not yet. Another spit of snow. The lines
of chaos, fractal patterns, atmosphere.
This change of shape, this change of entity,
a strangeness like the way I miss your feet,
the way my feet loved your feet in our bed.
The way I have no bed, no resting place.

On the Dangerous Way

In the white-flocked woods, shy trash,
like trillium. Late snow speckles the raw
mud lots. Big earthmovers rest on their treads;
archaeopteryx among guinea hens.

Slap of tires on slush and low click of termites
sucking stumps in the great cut forests;
passing methane gas.
Frost billows from a long brotherhood of trucks.

Eyes closed: the Chinese painting unrolls.
Tenuous bridge over mist to mountain;
one hairline path along the precipitous edge.
A single traveler climbs in the blowing snow.

Pamphlet for Bullfrogs

"O solo me oh," sang a gifted bullfrog on a dark spring evening.
His bass notes trembled with heavy importunance.
Many damsel frogs were jumping after mosquitoes.
"Hmm," said one damsel to another damsel,
"let's dive down and sit on the bottom.
It's getting noisy up here."
"What these frog experts don't tell us," said one bachelor,
"is how to handle the bull. Know what I mean?
Now you take my great-grandfather,
croaked right after his nuptials."
"When I was a tad, didn't have no more to worry about
than them wading herons," said another
as he leaped after the departing damsels.
"Its all froth on the beer," rumbled a puffed-out chest.
"Now all together, fellows,
let's give them a chorus they won't forget.
A one two, a one two… for he's a jolly green bellow
that nobody can but fry."

Storage

The human animal has turned a corner.
We no longer recognize one another.
I am the old species
but I must not weep. If I weep for myself
I am twice discarded.
"Don't weep," says the old brain,
"listen—I have it all on video
at half the price."

That's Not Me

I read that the left side
reveals the true self.
My true self has been
stitched to another face.
Not even my words fit.
I listen to what the
mouth is saying,
but I write in a small
notebook—
where is the body of
this person?

Every day the transit system
is a minute later.
The driver snores.
My feet move far away
in black plastic.

At night a thief enters.
Since then, the eyes in the mirror
are not mine.
Recently the nose
is unfamiliar.

Every day I am looking
for my face
among the faces that
I pass;
for my body,

a certain comfortable
size;
my voice, that even
now is not the one
that I remember.

Tell Me

"Tell me, Ruth, how is your vision?"
"Lord," I say, "know you not how it is with me?
You who are blind to the sorrows of all things temporal,
you who are not even the wind sliding under the door;
how is it that I hear this echo,
catching even in my blind eye the death throes of a distant star?"
And you say, voiceless as the forests of the mountains
of the Sahara, of the Gobi, of the Kalahari,
"Oom, ah, swept away."

The Apex

If there could be another time like that,
when all your ancestors and all of mine
conspired to bring us together. Back there
on the savanna in the days when we touched
the earth with our palms. Whose deep-set eyes
and heavy arms shoved all those others aside?

And yet, my love, you were so delicate. The flicker
of an almost infinite lightning, the infinitely small
leaping quanta, like the tracery of the universe
that was yourself, the strangeness of the animal.

The Barrier

Give back my brilliant ignorance.
Streets where I waited for you
in light waves,
in the cones of my eyes
the color of lost rooms;
those erotic odors.
Silence among the marble columns,
clash of mesh doors,
faded pretentious paper on the walls,
where we breathed in our bodies' acrid sweat
in the abyss of longing;
where we walked naked over the cheap carpets;
those casual rooms,
those pitiless hours.

The Gift from Isfahan

It is the vegetable dyes that were gathered and pounded and mixed.
It is the sheared wool carded and twisted.
It is the eyes and the fingers of children.
It is the threads tied knot by knot.
It is the daughters who carry it to the river.
It is the river that washes the skin and sweat from the patterns.
It is folded and wrapped in old cloths and sold for too little.
It is this that goes out to bless the feet of strangers.

This Is How It Is

I look at the gene bank,
examples by the millions,
and they won't do.
On this planet, for me,
there was only one impetuous specimen.
How angry I become
when I walk through the corridors of my dreams.
On all the beaches of the living world,
the shadows of where you were
are washed away by the tides.
Only in my skull,
night after night,
I wrestle with your obstinate ghost.
But even that is better
than this three-dimensional life
that is so boring without you.

The Cave

My mahjong eyes weep
when the sky weeps,
when color fades,
but it is the alphabet,
neat, succulent,
fresh slants of light
on the cave walls.
O skull, your hieroglyphs
shine far down
the passage,
as if the vapors
wrapped around
this spinning rock
were sweet as
lemon peel.

About the Author

Ruth Stone was born in Virginia in 1915. Her mother read Tennyson aloud while nursing her. She began writing poetry before the age of five, and since then has published thirteen volumes of poetry.

In 2002, Stone won the National Book Award and the Wallace Stevens Award from the Academy of American Poets for her book *In the Next Galaxy*. She has received many other awards and honors for her work, including the National Book Critics Circle Award, a Whiting Award, and two Guggenheim Fellowships, to name a few.

After the death of her husband in 1959, she raised their three daughters alone, while teaching at many universities.

She lives in Vermont, and her daughters live nearby.

The Chinese character for poetry is made up of two parts: "word" and "temple." It also serves as pressmark for Copper Canyon Press.

Since 1972, Copper Canyon Press has fostered the work of emerging, established, and world-renowned poets for an expanding audience. The Press thrives with the generous patronage of readers, writers, booksellers, librarians, teachers, students, and funders—everyone who shares the belief that poetry is vital to language and living.

Major funding has been provided by:

Anonymous (2)

Sarah and Tim Cavanaugh

Beroz Ferrell & The Point, LLC

Lannan Foundation

National Endowment for the Arts

Cynthia Lovelace Sears and Frank Buxton

Washington State Arts Commission

For information and catalogs:

COPPER CANYON PRESS
Post Office Box 271
Port Townsend, Washington 98368
360-385-4925
www.coppercanyonpress.org

Set in Charlotte Book, a typeface designed by Michael Gills and based roughly on type from eighteenth-century France by Pierre-Simon Fournier. Book design and composition by Valerie Brewster, Scribe Typography. Printed on archival-quality Glatfelter Author's Text at McNaughton & Gunn, Inc.